Houghton M...

Mathematics

MW00996565

Practice

5

HOUGHTON MIFFLIN

BOSTON • MORRIS PLAINS, NJ

California • Colorado • Georgia • Illinois • New Jersey • Texas

Contents

Chapter 1 1

Chapter 2 14

Chapter 3 25

Chapter 4 34

Chapter 5 50

Chapter 6 65

Chapter 7 79

Chapter 8 99

Chapter 9 109

Chapter 10 121

Chapter 11 139

Chapter 12 153

Name _____ Date _____

Place Value to Hundred Thousands

Write the value of each underlined digit in short word form.

Example
<u>8</u>4,592
80 thousand

1. <u>2</u>29,573

_____

2. 4<u>9</u>,134

_____

3. 8<u>4</u>,240

_____

4. 9<u>2</u>8,384

_____

5. <u>7</u>72,394

_____

Read each number. Then write it in short word form.

6. 84,304

_____

7. 832,403

_____

8. 93,735

_____

Write each number in standard form.

9. 40,000 + 7,000 + 500 + 30 + 1

_____

10. Four hundred eighty-nine thousand, three hundred four

_____

11. 800,000 + 4,000 + 300 + 20 + 8

_____

12. 76 thousand, 358

_____

Problem Solving • Reasoning

13. The earth is two hundred thirty-eight thousand, eight hundred fifty-seven miles from the moon. Write this distance in standard form.

_____

14. The earth measures 7,927 miles across. What is the value of each 7 in that number?

_____ _____

Name _____ Date _____

Exponents

Write each number in standard form.

> **Example**
>
> 6×10^4 **60,000**

1. 7×10^3 _____

2. $(4 \times 10^5) + (7 \times 10^4) + (4 \times 10^3) + (2 \times 10^2) + (3 \times 10^1) + (8 \times 10^0)$ _____

3. 4×10^3 _____ **4.** 3×10^4 _____ **5.** 7×10^1 _____

6. 8×10^2 _____ **7.** 1×10^4 _____ **8.** 5×10^5 _____

9. $(2 \times 10^3) + (7 \times 10^2) + (4 \times 10^1) + (3 \times 10^0)$ _____

10. $(5 \times 10^5) + (2 \times 10^3) + (9 \times 10^2) + (3 \times 10^0)$ _____

11. $(4 \times 10^5) + (2 \times 10^3) + (8 \times 10^1) + (9 \times 10^0)$ _____

Complete each pattern.

12. $4^5 = 1,024$
$4^4 = 256$
$4^3 = 64$
$4^2 = 16$
$4^1 =$ _____
$4^0 =$ _____

13. $729 \div 3 = 243$
$243 \div 3 = 81$
$81 \div 3 = 27$
$27 \div 3 = 9$
$9 \div 3 =$ _____
___ $\div 3 =$ _____

Problem Solving • Reasoning

14. Carrie is 2^3 years old and her brother Karl is 3^2 years old. Who is older? By how much?

_____

_____

15. If the base is 3, what exponent gives a value of 81?

_____

Name _____ Date _____

Compare, Order and Round Whole Numbers

<table>
<tr><td>

Example

85,930 ◯ 86,204

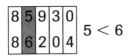

$5 < 6$

85,930 < 86,204

</td></tr>
</table>

Compare. Write >, <, or = for each ◯.

1. 842,948 ◯ 841,843   **2.** 48,394 ◯ 44,204

Order each set of numbers from least to greatest.

3. 98,845   482,951   92,843

_____   _____   _____

4. 313,518   82,549   215,846

_____   _____   _____

Round to the place of the underlined digit.

5. 3<u>1</u>2

_____

6. <u>8</u>,304

_____

7. 9<u>3</u>,704

_____

8. 516,<u>8</u>99

_____

9. 938,<u>4</u>83

_____

10. <u>5</u>16,849

_____

11. <u>4</u>8,519

_____

12. 51<u>7</u>,612

_____

Problem Solving • Reasoning

13. A toy company had a profit of $259,304 this year and $254,509 last year. Which profit was greater?

_____

14. Round this year's profit to the nearest ten thousand dollars.

_____

Name _____ Date _____

Problem-Solving Skill: Estimated or Exact Answers

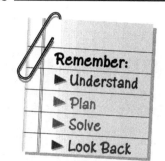

Remember:
► Understand
► Plan
► Solve
► Look Back

We use exact amounts when an amount can be counted or measured. We use an estimate for an amount that cannot be measured easily.

Use the report on stadiums to decide if an amount is estimated or exact.

> **Stadiums** Two of the world's largest sports stadiums are the Astrodome, in Houston, Texas, and the SkyDome, in Toronto, Ontario, Canada. The SkyDome can seat about 53,000 fans for a football game and about 67,000 people for a concert. The Astrodome can seat 63,001 fans for a football game. When the whole playing field is not needed (as for a boxing match), the Astrodome can accommodate as many as about 74,000 people. The most attended event ever at the SkyDome was Wrestlemania VI, held on April 1, 1990. 67,678 people attended that event.

1. 67,678 people attended Wrestlemania VI at the SkyDome.

   Think: Which amounts have been counted or measured?

   _____

2. The SkyDome can seat about 67,000 for a concert.

   Think: What word will tell you whether the amount is estimated or exact?

   _____

Choose a Strategy

Solve. Use these or other strategies.

Problem-Solving Strategies

| • Write an Equation | • Draw a Picture | • Find a Pattern | • Guess and Check |

3. How many dots make up the 5th triangle in this pattern?

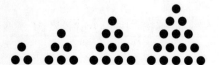

4. 5 children are sitting in a circle. Each child is connected to each other child by links of string. How many links of string are needed?

   _____

Name _____ Date _____

Millions and Billions

Write the value of the underlined digit in short word form.

Example
87<u>2</u>,483,558   **2 million**

1. 81,3<u>9</u>3,374,215 _____

2. 49<u>3</u>,481,402,414 _____

3. 549,<u>2</u>84,274,274 _____

4. 93,2<u>0</u>4,240,224 _____

Read the number. Then write it in short word form.

5. 352,502,305

_____

_____

6. 49,204,389,400

_____

_____

Write in standard form.

7. 4 billion, 35 million, 312 thousand, 4

_____

8. Three hundred twelve billion, four hundred thousand

_____

Order each set of numbers from least to greatest.

9. 823,402,203   91,309,372   182,392,346

_____

10. 549,284,274,274   81,284,280   93,204,240,224

_____

Problem Solving • Reasoning

11. A million is 1,000 thousands. What number is 100 hundreds? 10,000 ten-thousands?

_____ _____

12. Which is greater: 100 million or 10,000 hundred?

_____

Name _____ Date _____

Round Large Numbers

Round to the nearest million. Write the numbers in short word form.

Example
43,405,335 ——➤ 43 million

1. 84,483,382,401

2. 273,352,578,911

_____ _____

Round to the nearest billion. Write the numbers in short word form.

3. 4,593,204,193   **4.** 384,920,749,204   **5.** 79,687,634,011

_____ _____ _____

Round to the place of the underlined digit.

6. 7<u>8</u>1 _____   **7.** 7,<u>0</u>91 _____   **8.** 4<u>8</u>3,294 _____

9. 34,<u>2</u>04,274,482   **10.** 3<u>8</u>5,367,367,532   **11.** 8,2<u>0</u>5,473,593

_____ _____ _____

12. 485,248,5<u>8</u>8,249   **13.** 48,5<u>9</u>3,000,091   **14.** 539,9<u>9</u>9,981,302

_____ _____ _____

Problem Solving • Reasoning

15. In 1970, the world's population was about three billion, five hundred forty-eight million, four hundred fourteen thousand. Write this number in standard form and round it to the nearest hundred million.

16. By 1990, the world's population had reached about 5,115,510,000. Write this number in short word form and round it to the nearest billion.

_____

_____

_____ _____

Name _____ Date _____

Problem-Solving Strategy: Guess and Check

Remember:
► Understand
► Plan
► Solve
► Look Back

Solve each problem, using the Guess and Check strategy.

1. Charlotte has 3 times as many pencils in her schoolbox as Rebecca. Together, they have a total of 24 pencils. How many pencils does Rebecca have?

Think: What information should you start with?

_____

2. Joe delivers pizza. In his money pouch are 11 bills worth $39. If he has only $5 and $1 bills, how many of each type of bill does he have?

Think: Which types of bills are in Joe's money pouch?

_____

3. Rolanda's mom collects antique silverware. She has a total of 48 pieces. If she has twice as many spoons as all the other pieces combined, how many spoons does she have?

_____

4. There are 8 cars and motorcycles in the parking lot of FoodShop. If there are 24 wheels altogether, how many of each type of vehicle are there?

_____

Choose a Strategy

Solve. Use these or other strategies.

Problem-Solving Strategies			
• Draw a Picture	• Find a Pattern	• Guess and Check	• Make a Model

5. Haley's age is between 20 and 40. Her age is an even number which is divisible by 7. Find her age.

_____

6. 5 people meet for dinner at a restaurant. Each person shakes hands with every other person. How many handshakes were there?

_____

7. Mrs. Macmillan's 5th grade class has 24 students. There are half as many boys as girls. Find the number of boys in the class.

_____

8. The City Zoo charges $8 for adults and $4 for children. If a group of 10 people paid $48 for admission, how many adults were there?

_____

Name _____ Date _____

Place Value and Decimals

Example	**In words, what is the value of the underlined digit?**

Example

8.<u>4</u>5

The underlined digit has a value of four tenths.

In words, what is the value of the underlined digit?

1. 0.0<u>4</u>2 _____

2. 9.34<u>1</u> _____

3. 7.3<u>4</u>1 _____

4. 0.<u>6</u>5 _____

5. 4.6<u>8</u>0 _____

Make a place-value chart. Write each decimal in the chart and in words.

6. 7.301

7. 0.926

_____

8. 9.5

9. 82.08

_____

Write in standard form.

10. thirty-six thousandths _____

11. five and forty-two hundredths _____

12. sixty-eight and two hundred fourteen thousandths _____

13. eighty and three tenths _____

Problem Solving • Reasoning

14. In the State Track Championships, Carlos ran the 200 meter dash in 21.79 seconds. Write this decimal amount in words.

_____

_____

15. At the science museum, a laser measured Karen's height as forty-nine and seventeen thousandths inches. Write this height as a decimal.

_____

Name _____   Date _____

Compare and Order Decimals Less than One

Example
0.54 < 0.58

Compare. Write >, <, or = for each ◯.

1. 0.981 ◯ 0.082   **2.** 0.34 ◯ 0.340

3. 0.081 ◯ 0.81   **4.** 0.4 ◯ 0.08   **5.** 0.62 ◯ 0.70

6. 0.054 ◯ 0.54   **7.** 0.900 ◯ 0.9   **8.** 0.811 ◯ 0.099

Order each set of numbers from greatest to least.

9. 0.032 0.90 0.088   **10.** 0.54 0.82 0.61   **11.** 0.488 0.048 0.15

_____   _____   _____

12. 0.25 0.065 0.84 0.4   **13.** 0.215 0.24 0.241 0.284

_____   _____

14. 0.255 0.248 0.251 0.018   **15.** 0.215 0.051 0.008 0.542

_____   _____

Problem Solving • Reasoning

16. Precious jewels are measured in carats. A jeweler has a ruby weighing 0.627 carats, a diamond weighing 0.82 carats and a pearl weighing 0.092 carats. List the jewels in order from heaviest to lightest.

_____

17. The jeweler has two sapphires. One weighs 0.94 carats. The other weighs 0.099 carats. Write a number sentence using >, < or = to compare the two weights.

_____

Name _____   Date _____

Round Decimals

Example
3.58 rounds to **3.6**

Round to the nearest tenth.

1. 0.159 _____   **2.** 0.002 _____   **3.** 5.451 _____

4. 5.21 _____   **5.** 8.517 _____   **6.** 0.87 _____   **7.** 9.99 _____

Round to the nearest hundredth.

8. 0.551 _____   **9.** 0.761 _____   **10.** 0.849 _____

11. 3.518 _____   **12.** 2.0518 _____   **13.** 5.2184 _____

14. 13.5176 _____   **15.** 84.510 _____

Round to the nearest whole number.

16. 3.24 _____   **17.** 9.59 _____   **18.** 6.31 _____   **19.** 25.8 _____

20. 5.6 _____   **21.** 8.138 _____   **22.** 5.849 _____   **23.** 3.99 _____

Problem Solving • Reasoning

24. John's teacher is calculating math test averages. John's average is 88.38. Round this average to the nearest whole number.

25. To qualify for the Math Team, John's average must be greater than 88.5 when rounded to the nearest tenth. Does John qualify? Explain.

Name _____ Date _____

Compare and Order Decimals and Whole Numbers

Example
1.15 > 1.015

Compare. Write >, <, or =.

1. 22 ⟨<⟩ 22.519   **2.** 4,265 ⟨=⟩ 4,265

3. 5.315 ⟨<⟩ 6   **4.** 4.56 ⟨<⟩ 45.6   **5.** 23.99 ⟨>⟩ 2.399

6. 8.150 ⟨=⟩ 8.15   **7.** 85.516 ⟨<⟩ 85.651   **8.** 5.550 ⟨=⟩ 5.55

Order each set of numbers from greatest to least.

9. 0.52 5.2 0.052
5.2, 0.52, 0.052

10. 6 5.2 6.51
6.51, 6, 5.2

11. 0.81 8.10 8.01
8.10, 8.01, 0.81

12. 0.42 0.94 0.49
0.94, 0.49, 0.42

13. 0.485 0.082 0.762
0.762, 0.485, 0.082

14. 0.452 0.052 0.254
0.452, 0.254, 0.052

15. 0.64 6.40 6.04 0.46
6.40, 6.04, 0.64, 0.46

16. 1.25 5 7.1 0.64
7.1, 5, 1.25, 0.64

17. 0.2 2 0.24 0.244
2, 0.244, 0.24, 0.2

Problem Solving • Reasoning

18. At the State Track & Field Championships, Rodney threw the shot put 13.09 meters and 13.42 meters. Which throw was longer?
13.42

19. At the track meet, Rebecca's time in the 1-mile race was 8.821 minutes. Last year her time was 8.809 minutes. In which year did she have a faster time?
8.809

Name _____   Date _____

Negative Numbers and the Number Line

Example
⁻4 < 3.5

Compare. Draw a number line from ⁻4.5 to 4.5 and label each 0.5 unit. Write >, <, or = for each ◯.

1. 4 ⬭> -2

2. ⁻3 ⬭> ⁻4

3. ⁻1 ⬭< 4.5

4. 2.5 ⬭> ⁻2.5

5. 3.5 ⬭= 3.5

6. 3.5 ◯ ⁻4

7. 3.5 ◯ 2.5

8. ⁻2 ◯ 0

9. ⁻0.5 ◯ ⁻1.5

10. 0 ◯ ⁻2.5

11. 0.5 ◯ ⁻1

12. ⁻3.5 ⬭= ⁻3.5

13. ⁻1 ◯ ⁻1

14. 2 ◯ ⁻3

15. 1.5 ◯ ⁻1.5

16. ⁻3 ◯ 4

17. 0.5 ◯ ⁻0.5

18. ⁻3.5 ◯ ⁻2

19. 3 ◯ 2.5

20. ⁻3 ◯ 0

21. ⁻3 ◯ ⁻3.5

22. 1 ◯ 3.5

23. ⁻2 ◯ ⁻1

24. 0 ◯ 4

Problem Solving • Reasoning

25. The high temperatures for three days in January were 4°, -3°, and -1°. Order these temperatures from greatest to least.

_____

26. What temperature is 7 degrees colder than 3°?

_____

Name _____   Date _____

Problem-Solving Application: Use a Table

Make and use a table to solve each problem.

1. Eloise's class is having an ice cream sundae party. There are 5 different toppings: sprinkles, whipped cream, hot fudge sauce, candy bits, and peanuts. How many different sundaes can Eloise make using 2 different toppings?

   Think: How many combinations of 2 toppings are there?

   _____

2. Isabel found some quarters and dimes when she cleaned under the couch. She counted the money and found that there is $1.15. How many of each type of coin did she find under the couch?

   Think: What is a reasonable number of coins to make $1.15?

   _____

3. Jeremiah bought a shirt for $19.40. He gave the clerk a $20 bill and got 4 coins in change. What coins was he given?

   _____

4. Hector can choose any 4 of the 5 screensavers offered with his new computer. How many different combinations of 4 screensavers could he choose?

   _____

Choose a Strategy

Solve. Use these or other strategies.

Problem-Solving Strategies

• Guess and Check	• Make a Model	• Draw a Picture	• Find a Pattern

5. Tyler has 8 pets. If his chickens and dogs have a total of 26 legs, how many of each type of animal does he have?

   _____

6. Three lines pass through a circle and cut it into pieces. What is the greatest number of pieces which can be formed?

   _____

7. For how many numbers less than 100 is the digit in the ones place half the digit in the tens place?

   _____

8. Last week Amy's basketball team scored 8 points more than twice the number they scored this week. If they scored 14 points this week, how many did they score last week?

   _____

Name _____ Date _____

Add Whole Numbers

Add. Estimate to check that your answer is reasonable.

Example
1
325
+905
1,230

1. 282
  +633

2. 177
  +600

3. 999
  +521

4. 468
  +934

5. 5,691
  +3,953

6. 3,873
  +5,116

7. 6,233
  +2,276

8. 745
  +1,542

9. 2,785
  +7,926

10. 8,113
  +2,642

11. 1,025
  +5,841

12. 4,125
  +18,166

13. 6,422
  +61,988

14. 58,745
  +89,622

Algebra • Patterns

Find each sum when $n = 1,000,000$.

15. $n + 5$

16. $n + 5,000$

17. $n + 5,000,000$

_____ _____ _____

Problem Solving • Reasoning

18. Zach has 4,213 baseball cards. His parents gave him 349 more as a birthday present. Now, how many baseball cards does Zach have?

_____

19. At the beginning of a music concert, 41,516 people were there. After the first half, 2,942 more people came. How many total people attended the concert?

_____

Name _____   Date _____

Subtract Whole Numbers

Subtract. Add to check your answer.

Example

$$\begin{array}{r} {}^{4}\,{}^{12}\,{}^{11} \\ 5\,3\,1\!\!\!/ \\ -1\,7\,7 \\ \hline 3\,5\,4 \end{array}$$

1. 791
    −393

2. 3,100
    − 622

3. 8,243
    −2,333

4. 4,512
    −4,177

5. 3,873
    − 600

6. 4,125
    −1,542

7. 999
    −934

8. 62,877
    − 6,421

9. 7,923
    −4,177

10. 66,531
    −20,111

11. 1,567
    − 742

12. 5,952
    − 583

13. 30,134
    −24,868

14. 38,529
    − 880

15. 357 − 56

16. 5,921 − 5,018

17. 4,338 − 291

Problem Solving • Reasoning

18. When Mr. Noble's class put all their pennies together, they had 738 pennies. Kris had donated 250 pennies. How many were donated by the other students?

19. Sam has to write a 5,000-word paper about a foreign country. He has written 2,143 words so far. How many more words does he have to write?

Name _____   Date _____

Problem-Solving Skill: Too Much or Too Little Information

Solve each if you can. If a problem is incomplete, tell what information you would need to solve it.

1. At the farm show, there were 322 sheep and 57 cows in Building A, 402 pigs and 28 cows in Building B, and 89 pigs in Building C. How many animals were in the three buildings altogether?

Think: Which numbers in the problem tell how many animals there were?

_____

2. The farm show began at 9:00 a.m. and closed at 10:00 p.m. The information booth at the show was open from 8:00 a.m. to 11:00 p.m. The parking lot is open all day and night. How many hours longer is the information booth open than the show?

Think: Is there too much or too little information in this problem?

_____

Choose a Strategy

Solve each if you can. Choose these or other strategies. If a problem is incomplete, tell what information you would need to solve it.

Problem-Solving Strategies

- Draw a Picture   • Guess and Check   • Make a Table   • Too Much/Too Little Information

3. For the country music concert, 3,211 tickets were sold but only 3,067 people attended the concert. Toward the end, it began to rain and 2,889 people left the concert. How many people were left at the end of the concert?

_____

4. At the refreshment stand, 500 people bought ice cream and 289 people bought lemonade. Lemonade cost $2.00 for each cup. Was more money spent on ice cream than on lemonade?

_____

_____

Name _____ Date _____

Add Decimals

Add. Estimate to check that your answer is reasonable.

Example
$4.56
+ 6.32
$10.88

1. 7.59
    +2.09

2. 4.88
    +6.76

3. $7.50
    + 3.87

4. 9.01
    +3.73

5. 25.9
    +34.8

6. 157.8
    + 30.1

7. 245.0
    + 8.931

8. 57.14
    + 3.689

9. $8.55
    + 7.49

10. 83.041
     + 5.226

11. 15.8
     46.9
    +145.733

12. 635.33
      9.338
    +   0.994

13. 5.001
    64.893
    +158.6

14. 145.2
    452.8
    + 68.44

15. 153.7 + 1.4

16. 61.108 + 6.22

17. 49.20 + 5.81 + .854

18. A relay race consisted of three sections. Team A finished the first section in 124.5 seconds, the second in 165.98 seconds and the third in 89.243 seconds. How much time did it take Team A to run the race?

19. Kyle helped his mom weigh fruit and vegetables at the grocery store. The potatoes weighed 6.42 pounds. The watermelon weighed 15.87 pounds. How much do the potatoes and watermelon weigh together?

Name _____   Date _____

Subtract Decimals

Subtract. Add to check your answer.

Example

$$\begin{array}{r} {\scriptstyle 4\ 17} \\ \not{5}.\not{7}8 \\ -3.82 \\ \hline 1.96 \end{array}$$

1.
$$\begin{array}{r} 10.42 \\ -\ 6.01 \\ \hline \end{array}$$

2.
$$\begin{array}{r} \$52.90 \\ -\ 25.00 \\ \hline \end{array}$$

3.
$$\begin{array}{r} 18.45 \\ -\ 5.10 \\ \hline \end{array}$$

4.
$$\begin{array}{r} 14.07 \\ -\ 2.88 \\ \hline \end{array}$$

5.
$$\begin{array}{r} \$19.99 \\ -\ 12.70 \\ \hline \end{array}$$

6.
$$\begin{array}{r} 84.26 \\ -76.48 \\ \hline \end{array}$$

7.
$$\begin{array}{r} 17.04 \\ -\ 5.32 \\ \hline \end{array}$$

8.
$$\begin{array}{r} \$46.00 \\ -\ 5.00 \\ \hline \end{array}$$

9.
$$\begin{array}{r} 90.82 \\ -32.74 \\ \hline \end{array}$$

10.
$$\begin{array}{r} 36.53 \\ -\ 4.52 \\ \hline \end{array}$$

11.
$$\begin{array}{r} \$6.98 \\ -\ 4.18 \\ \hline \end{array}$$

12.
$$\begin{array}{r} 58.00 \\ -42.64 \\ \hline \end{array}$$

13.
$$\begin{array}{r} 19.44 \\ -\ 1.39 \\ \hline \end{array}$$

14.
$$\begin{array}{r} 99.42 \\ -77.02 \\ \hline \end{array}$$

15. $4.45 - 3.29$

16. $17.89 - 6.52$

17. $57.46 - 25.43$

18. The temperature yesterday was 84.6 degrees. Today it was 76.0 degrees. How much cooler is it today than yesterday?

19. Jill earned $56.42 over the summer. She wants to spend $16.99 on a new CD. After she buys the CD, how much money will she have left?

Name _____ Date _____

Problem-Solving Strategy: Work Backward

Solve each problem using the Work Backward strategy.

1. The concession stand sold 36 cans of juice. There were 13 fewer cans of soda sold than cans of juice and 10 fewer bottles of water sold than cans of soda. How many bottles of water were sold?

> **Think:** What information will you start with?

_____

2. During track season, Scott won 4 more races than John. Bryan won 1 more race than Scott. Casey won 2 fewer races than Bryan. John won 3 races. How many races did each boy win?

> **Think:** Which boy should you start with? Why?

_____

_____

Choose a Strategy

Solve. Use these or other strategies.

Problem-Solving Strategies

- Find a Pattern
- Draw a Diagram
- Too Much/Too Little Information
- Work Backward

3. Jill scored a total of 12 points in the last basketball game. She scored twice as many points in the second half of the game as she did in the first half. How many points did she score in each half?

_____

_____

4. A total of 2,347 people attended the basketball game. Student tickets are $2.50 and adult tickets are $4.00. How many students attended the game?

_____

_____

5. The basketball coach bought 128 uniforms. If 60 of them were girls' uniforms and 4 were coaches' uniforms. How many boys' uniforms were bought?

_____

6. During practice, Kim ran 0.25 more miles than Jan. Liz ran 1.5 miles less than Kim. Liz ran 3 miles. How many miles did Kim and Jan run?

_____

Name _____   Date _____

Expressions and Equations

Simplify.

Example
6 + (8 − 3)
6 + 5 = **11**

1. 25 + (16 − 4)

_____

2. (9 + 15) − 11

_____

3. (14 − 11) + 5

_____

4. 18 − (6 + 7)

_____

5. 8.5 + (12 − 4)

_____

6. 4.3 − (1.2 + 2)

_____

7. 55 − (23 + 20)

_____

8. 13.4 + (6.82 − 3.009)

_____

9. 13.7 − (1.22 + 2.2) + 2

_____

10. (9 − 1) + (11 + 7)

_____

Write >, <, or = for each ◯ **.**

11. (6 + 17) − 13 ◯ 6 + (17 − 13)

12. (2.67 − 0.17) + 1.3 ◯ 2.67 − (0.17 + 1.3)

13. (40 − 12) + 6 ◯ 30 − (5 + 8)

14. 6.92 + (20.08 − 12.52) ◯ (29.65 − 12.48) − 5.21

Problem Solving • Reasoning

15. Jack spent a day at an amusement park. He started with $45.25. He spent $11.44 on food and $25.50 on entrance into the park. How much money does he have left?

_____

16. Sasha spent $0.89 on a drink and $0.25 on an apple. Nell spent $1.59 on some crackers. Which girl spent more money? How much more?

_____

Name _____ Date _____

Write and Evaluate Expressions

Example
Subtract a number from 9
$9 - n$

Write an algebraic expression for each word phrase. Use the variable *n* to represent the unknown number.

1. 17 plus a number

_____

2. 45 less than a number

_____

3. Take away a number from 3

_____

4. 31 is increased by a number

_____

5. 14 more than a number

_____

6. A number plus 8

_____

Write each algebraic expression in words.

7. $3 + n$ _____

8. $70 - g$ _____

9. $p + 26$ _____

10. $x - 15$ _____

Evaluate each expression when $x = 15$ and $y = 1$.

11. $(11 + x) - y$

_____

12. $(x - 8) + 4$

_____

13. $7 - 2 + (x + y)$

14. $(24 - x) + y - 5$

_____

Problem Solving • Reasoning

15. In Mrs. Jennings class, there are 13 boys and some girls. Write an algebraic expression that describes the number of students in the class.

_____

16. Josh had some money. He bought a T-shirt for $14. Write an algebraic expression that describes how much money Josh has left.

_____

Name _____   Date _____

Write and Solve Equations

Solve and check.

Example
$5 + x = 17$
$x = 17 - 5$
$x = \mathbf{12}$

1. $p + 6 = 11$

_____

2. $19 + z = 28$

_____

3. $n + 8 = 33$

_____

4. $12 + e = 19$

_____

5. $g + 7 = 32$

_____

6. $21 + v = 41$

_____

7. $b + 38 = 45$

_____

8. $36 - p = 14$

_____

9. $x - 4 = 53$

_____

10. $10 - y = 2$

_____

11. $a - 6 = 64$

_____

12. $5 - p = 3$

_____

13. $n - 78 = 39$

_____

14. $84 - m = 52$

_____

15. $z - 22 = 79$

_____

16. $11.2 - c = 4$

_____

17. $q - 80 = 49$

_____

18. $68 + k = 92$

_____

19. $t + 37 = 79$

_____

Problem Solving • Reasoning

Write an equation to solve each problem.

20. Tom and Rick put their money together to buy a game. Together they had $14.56. If Rick contributed $4.33, how much did Tom contribute?

_____

_____

21. Shannon had a coupon for popcorn at the movies. The original price of the popcorn was $3.10. Shannon only had to pay $1.75. What was the value of the coupon?

_____

_____

Name _____ Date _____

Model the Distributive Property

Example

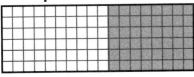

$6 \times 10 = 60$
$6 \times 8 = 48$
$60 + 48 = 108$
$6 \times 18 = 108$

List the partial products for each and find their sum.
Then write a multiplication sentence for each.

1.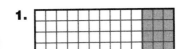

_____   _____

_____   _____

2.

_____

_____

_____

_____

3.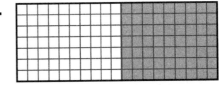

_____

_____

_____

_____

Draw and divide a rectangle to show each product.
Use the Distributive Property to find the product.

4. 4×18

5. 7×21

_____   _____

_____   _____

Name _____   Date _____

Multiply by a One-Digit Number

Example
$\overset{1\ 2}{247}$ $\times\ \ \ 4$ $\overline{\ 988\ }$

Multiply. Estimate to check that your answer is reasonable.

1. 63
$\times\ 7$

2. 89
$\times\ 5$

3. 561
$\times\ \ \ 9$

4. 67
$\times\ 4$

5. 29
$\times\ 7$

6. 846
$\times\ \ \ 5$

7. $14.22
$\times\ \ \ \ \ 3$

8. 714
$\times\ \ \ 8$

9. 973
$\times\ \ \ 2$

10. 727
$\times\ \ \ 3$

11. 398
$\times\ \ \ 6$

12. 669
$\times\ \ \ 5$

13. 2,393
$\times\ \ \ \ \ 7$

14. 4,352
$\times\ \ \ \ \ 8$

15. 7,516
$\times\ \ \ \ \ 4$

Problem Solving • Reasoning

16. A dragonfly can fly 36 miles in one hour. How far can it fly in 5 hours?

_____

17. Sara needs four notebooks for school. How much will the notebooks cost altogether if each one costs $3.29?

_____

Name _____   Date _____

Multiply with Zeros

Example
$\overset{2}{3}07$ $\times\ \ 4$ **1,228**

Multiply. Check your answer by estimating.

1. 603
     $\times\ \ 4$

2. 801
     $\times\ \ 6$

3. 506
     $\times\ \ 9$

4. 4 × 607

5. 2 × 308

6. 8 × 406

7. 6 × $3.02

8. 54,203 x 6

9. 4,301 x 8

10. 54,008 x 2

11. 4,304 x 9

Problem Solving • Reasoning

12. Veronica is paid $8.07 per hour. If she works 5 hours this week, how much will she be paid?

13. When full, a cruise ship can hold 1,805 people. If the ship makes 7 voyages and is full each time, how many people have been on the ship?

Name _____ Date _____

Problem-Solving Skill: Estimated or Exact Answers

Answer by estimating or calculating.

1. Charlene goes to the store with $40.00. She needs to buy 7 beach towels for $6.75 each. Will she have enough money?

Think: How can I be sure that an estimate will not be greater than the actual product?

_____

2. If Charlene decides to buy only 3 beach towels, what will her change be from $40.00?

Think: Should I use an estimate or calculate the exact amount to find the total cost and amount of change?

_____

3. How much more change would Charlene receive if the 3 beach towels had been on sale for $5.50 each?

_____

4. Charlene and her 6 friends want to line their towels up next to each other. If each towel is 34 inches wide, will the towels fit onto a pool deck which is 300 inches wide?

_____

Choose a Strategy

Solve. Use these or other strategies.

Problem-Solving Strategies

| • Make a Model | • Draw a Diagram | • Find a Pattern | • Solve a Simpler Problem |

5. The temperature on Monday was 77 degrees. If the temperature decreases 3 degrees each day, what will the temperature be on Friday?

_____

6. Sam can choose among 3 flavors of ice cream, 2 toppings, and 3 types of candy for his ice cream sundae. How many different sundaes are possible?

_____

7. Ursula bought 82 floor tiles for $86.36. The next week, they went on sale for $45.36. How much would she have saved buying the tiles on sale?

_____

8. At a round table with 5 chairs, Ron is sitting to Kim's right, and Jo is sitting to Kim's left. Jo is sitting between Alex and Kim, and May sits two chairs away from Kim. Who sits to Alex's left?

_____

Name _____ Date _____

Mental Math: Multiply Multiples of 10, 100 and 1,000

Example
600
× 30
18,000

Use mental math to find each product.

1. 70
      × 8

2. 30
      × 9

3. 600
      × 8

4. 400
      × 8

5. 6,000
      ×   5

6. 4,000
      ×   9

7. 8,000
      ×   8

8. 70 × 70

_____

9. 20 × 80

_____

10. 80 × 500

_____

11. 500 × 20

_____

12. 20 × 400

_____

13. 30 × 900

_____

14. 40 × 6,000

_____

15. 80 × 2,000

_____

Choose the greater product without multiplying first. Use > or < for each ◯.

16. 50 × 30 ◯ 6 × 700

17. 400 × 90 ◯ 900 × 50

Problem Solving • Reasoning

18. A jet airplane can travel at 400 miles per hour. How far could the jet travel in 6 hours?

_____

19. The human heart pumps about 2,000 gallons of blood in one day. How many gallons does it pump in 30 days?

_____

Name _____   Date _____

Multiplying by Multiples of 10

Example
48
$\times$40   Think: 40 = 4 $\times$ 10
???
48
$\times$ 4
192
192 $\times$ 10 = 1,920
So, 48 $\times$ 40 = **1,920**

Multiply.

1. 88
$\times$20

2. 61
$\times$40

3. 45
$\times$70

4. 47
$\times$20

5. 55
$\times$60

6. 547
$\times$30

7. 314 x 40

_____

8. 846 x 40

_____

9. 254 x 70

_____

10. 398 x 20

_____

11. 621 x 50

_____

12. 5,122 x 10

_____

13. 1,728 x 30

_____

14. 2,612 x 20

_____

Problem Solving • Reasoning

15. Ed and his brother are participating in a bike-a-thon for charity. For 15 days, they will bike 40 miles each day. How far will they bike altogether?

_____

16. A car dealer pays an average of $5,691 for each of 40 used cars. How much does she pay altogether?

_____

Name _____ Date _____

Problem-Solving Strategy: Write an Equation

Write an equation for each problem.

1. Hanna says she is four years older than twice her brother's age. If she is 18 years old, how old is her brother?

> **Think:** What is the equation for this problem?

_____

2. Iris' baby brother was born 3 weeks plus some number of days ago. If the baby is 25 days old, what is the missing number?

> **Think:** How many days are in a week?

_____

3. If Tasha finds that 3 ounces of shampoo lasts for 27 days, how many ounces will she need for 63 days?

_____

4. Joanne thinks of the number of siblings she has. When she multiplies the number by 7 and adds 2, she gets 23. How many siblings does Joanne have?

_____

Choose a Strategy

Solve. Use these or other strategies.

Problem-Solving Strategies

- Guess and Check   • Use a Table   • Work Backward   • Write an Equation

5. Some cars and motorcycles are parked in Sara's driveway. There are 3 times as many cars as motorcycles, and there are a total of 28 tires. How many motorcycles are there?

_____

6. Find a rule that changes each number in the top row into the number below. Use the rule to fill in the missing numbers.

2	3	4	6	8	9
3	5	___	11	___	___

7. Carla started with some number of trading cards. She gave away 13 and received four. After that, she threw away one half of her collection, leaving 40 cards. How many cards did she start with?

_____

8. The width of a rectangle is 4 more than its length. If the perimeter is 28 inches, what are its length and width?

_____ _____

Name _____ Date _____

Multiply by Two-Digit Numbers

Example
$\overset{1}{1}\overset{1}{\cancel{2}}$ 147 $\times 24$ —— 588 $+2940$ —— **3,528**

Multiply. Estimate to check.

1.   63
   $\times 74$

2.   86
   $\times 51$

3.   35
   $\times 49$

4. $0.45
   $\times\ \ 37$

5. $3.62
   $\times\ \ 28$

6.   27
   $\times 81$

7.   822
   $\times\ \ 48$

8. $0.64 × 86

9. 853 × 41

10. 214 × 73

11. $7.15 × 48

_____   _____   _____   _____

Problem Solving • Reasoning

12. There are 62 windows on each floor of a skyscraper which is 43 stories tall. How many windows are there altogether?

13. Fran's class went to the zoo. Each of the 26 children in her class paid the $4.25 admission fee. How much did it cost for the entire class to go to the zoo?

_____   _____

Name _____ Date _____

Find the Mean

**Find the mean. Compare with the set of numbers
to make sure the answer is reasonable.**

Example	
17, 17, 19, 20, 22	17 17 19 20 +22 95 95 ÷ 5 = 19
The mean is **19**.	

1. 78, 77, 82, 83, 71, 71

_____

2. 270, 305, 325

_____

3. 24, 26, 30, 35, 35

_____

4. 62, 67, 68, 103

_____

5. 12, 19, 21, 28, 30

_____

6. 45, 67, 83, 100, 105

_____

Problem Solving • Reasoning

7. Sara's spelling scores for the month of
January were: 88, 89, 90, 93 and 95. What
was Sara's mean spelling score for the
month of January?

_____

8. Mike earned $25 mowing lawns last
week. The previous four weeks he earned
$12, $20, $25 and $23. What is the mean
amount Mike earned mowing lawns?

_____

Name _____   Date _____

Problem-Solving Skill: Interpret Remainders

Solve.

1. The fifth grade students are putting on a play. The costumes require 2 yards of fabric per costume. How many costumes can be made with 45 yards of fabric?

    Think: Can a costume be made with less than 2 yards of fabric?

   _____

2. The 112 students in the play are divided into groups of 6 plus one smaller group. How many students are in the smaller group?

   Think: Will the answer be less than 6 or more than 6?

   _____

3. The cafeteria supplied juice for the performers. If each container holds 9 cups of juice, and the students drank a total of 140 cups of juice, how many full containers of juice did the students drink?

   _____

4. Jennifer had 500 programs. She gave each of 6 helpers an equal number of programs to hand out and left the remaining programs in the room. How many programs did she leave in the room?

   _____

Choose a Strategy.

Solve. Use these or other strategies.

Problem-Solving Strategies

• Guess and Check	• Work Backward	• Write an Equation	• Make a Table

5. A photographer took 140 pictures of the students during the play, and filled several display boards with the photos. If each display board holds 9 photos, how many display boards were filled with photos?

   _____

6. The students sold 115 tickets for students at $2.50 each, 47 tickets for children at $1.50 each and 232 tickets for adults at $5.00 each. How many total tickets were sold?

   _____

Name _____   Date _____

Divide by Multiples of 10, 100, and 1,000

Divide. Use mental math. Check by multiplying.

Example
450 ÷ 50
45 ÷ 5 = 9
450 ÷ 50 = **9**

1. 12,000 ÷ 60

_____

2. 600 ÷ 20

_____

3. 30,000 ÷ 1,000

_____

4. 250 ÷ 25

_____

5. 72,000 ÷ 900

_____

6. 8,100 ÷ 90

_____

7. 360 ÷ 60

_____

8. 21,000 ÷ 300

_____

9. 640,000 ÷ 800

_____

10. 40,000 ÷ 5,000

_____

11. 560,000 ÷ 8

_____

Problem Solving • Reasoning

12. There are a total of 10,000 students in the Middledale school district. If there are 20 students per classroom, how many classrooms are in the Middledale school district?

_____

13. In Langley, there is one building principal for every 500 students. Langley School District has 4,000 students. How many building principals are there?

_____

Name _____   Date _____

Divide by Two-Digit Numbers

Divide.

Example
12 R32
45)572
45
‾‾‾
122
90
‾‾‾
32

1. 23)865

2. 80)576

3. 31)478

4. 26)198

5. 37)255

6. 29)896

7. 56)582

8. 78)210

9. 38)739

10. 12)845

11. 29)529

12. $281 \div 17$

13. $927 \div 43$

14. $77 \div 14$

15. $82 \div 41$

Problem Solving • Reasoning

16. There are 368 new books to be distributed evenly to the 23 classrooms in the elementary school. How many books will each classroom get?

17. The students distributing the books carry them on a cart that holds 34 books at a time. How many trips will they need to make to deliver all 368 books?

Name _____ Date _____

Estimated Quotient Is Too Large

Divide.

Example
**5 R29**$$**Think:** $300 \div 50 = 6$
$52\overline{)289}$
260
29

1. $43\overline{)335}$ $\qquad$ **2.** $87\overline{)536}$

3. $34\overline{)211}$ $\qquad$ **4.** $45\overline{)839}$ $\qquad$ **5.** $64\overline{)319}$ $\qquad$ **6.** $35\overline{)574}$

7. $92\overline{)713}$ $\qquad$ **8.** $56\overline{)812}$ $\qquad$ **9.** $73\overline{)431}$ $\qquad$ **10.** $98\overline{)360}$

11. $575 \div 29$ $\qquad$ **12.** $625 \div 82$ $\qquad$ **13.** $805 \div 94$ $\qquad$ **14.** $589 \div 23$

_____ _____ _____ _____

Problem Solving • Reasoning

15. The bike shop ordered 1,170 water bottles to sell. The water bottles were delivered in 13 large boxes. How many water bottles were in each box?

16. A total of 837 customers visited the bike shop in May. That month, the store was open 27 days. If an equal number of customers came in each day, how many customers visited the bike shop each day in May?

_____ _____

Name _____   Date _____

Estimated Quotient Is Too Small

Divide.

Example
$$\begin{array}{r} 5\ \text{R4} \\ 27\overline{)139} \\ -135 \\ \hline 4 \end{array}$$

1. $28\overline{)224}$ **2.** $16\overline{)121}$ **3.** $45\overline{)689}$

4. $26\overline{)229}$ **5.** $75\overline{)267}$ **6.** $85\overline{)178}$ **7.** $35\overline{)286}$

8. $46\overline{)445}$ **9.** $65\overline{)793}$ **10.** $36\overline{)309}$ **11.** $74\overline{)487}$

Problem Solving • Reasoning

12. Mark volunteered at the public library this summer. He worked 35 days, and in those days he checked in 1,960 books. If he checked in an equal number of books each day, how many did he check in each day?

13. At the library, in 26 days, 1,560 people checked out books. Each person checked out one book. What is the average number of books checked out per day?

Name _____ Date _____

Four- and Five-Digit Dividends

Divide.

Example
496 R11 16)7947 64 154 144 107 96 11

1. 39)5,682

2. 42)35,874

3. 56)2,765

4. 16)91,265

5. 47)8,795

6. 9,823 ÷ 23

7. 23,498 ÷ 30

8. 45,720 ÷ 34

_____

_____

_____

Problem Solving • Reasoning

9. There are 35,868 corn plants in a field. If the field is planted in 98 even rows, how many corn plants are in each row?

10. The farm has 57 rows of soybean plants. If there are a total of 14,250 soybean plants, how many soybean plants are in each row?

_____

_____

Name _____ Date _____

Problem-Solving Strategy: Draw a Diagram

Draw a diagram to solve each problem.

1. The grocery store stocks 180 types of produce. There are 5 types of fruit for every 4 types of vegetables. How many types of fruit and vegetables does the store stock?

   Think: How many items does each rectangle represent?

   _____

2. The grocery store employs cashiers and grocery baggers. There are 24 baggers. There are 12 more cashiers than baggers. How many cashiers are there?

   Think: How can I find the number of cashiers first?

   _____

3. There are two types of carts at the grocery store; those with child seats and those without. There are 9 carts without child seats for every cart with a child seat. There are 500 carts at the store, how many do not have child seats?

   _____

4. The grocery store stocks 3 brands of yogurt. The store sells two containers of Brand A yogurt for every one container of Brand B or Brand C yogurt. If the store sells 100 containers of yogurt a day, how much of each brand of yogurt do they sell?

   _____

Choose a Strategy.

Solve. Use these or other strategies.

Problem-Solving Strategies

• Draw a diagram	• Make a Table	• Work Backward	• Write an Equation

5. Mark went to the grocery store to buy 3 bottles of fruit juice. The juice costs $1.30 per bottle. How much change should Mark receive if he pays for the juice with $5.00?

   _____

6. The grocery store stocks three kinds of crackers. The costs of the different brands of crackers are $1.29, $1.59, and $1.47 per box. What is the mean cost of a box of crackers from the store?

   _____

Name _____ Date _____

Write and Evaluate Expressions

Write each word phrase as an algebraic expression.

Example
A number minus three.
(x − 3)

1. 10 times a number

_____

2. 3 more than 3 times a number

3. 4 less than a number

_____ _____

Write each algebraic expression in words.

4. $t - 19$ **5.** $3x + 2$ **6.** $8 \div (m + 4)$

_____ _____ _____

Evaluate each expression.

7. $3t - 2$, if $t = 3$ **8.** $(6b) + 4$, if $b = 1$ **9.** $(15 \div x) - 2$, if $x = 3$

_____ _____ _____

Problem Solving • Reasoning

10. Maria can deliver 42 newspapers in an hour. Write an expression that shows how long it would take her to deliver 126 newspapers.

11. Maria earns $5.25 for each hour she works. This month she received a $20.00 bonus. Write an expression to show how much money she earned this month.

_____ _____

Name _____ Date _____

Write and Solve Equations

Solve by using any method.

Example
$52 = 4k$
$k = 13$

1. $t \div 7 = 10$

_____

2. $d \div 3 = 5$

_____

3. $s \div 8 = 3$

_____

4. $12 = 2m$

_____

5. $81 \div p = 9$

_____

6. $100 \div n = 25$

_____

7. $12h = 132$

_____

8. $55s = 165$

_____

9. $3 \div r = 1$

_____

10. $99 = 11t$

_____

11. $r \div 2 = 17$

_____

Write and solve an equation for each situation.

12. 12 books on each shelf times the number of shelves equals 144 books.

_____

13. The number of pages per book times 100 books equals 6,200 pages.

_____

Problem Solving • Reasoning

14. Georgiana is planning a reception. Each table seats 6 people. How many tables will she need for each number of guests?

   a. 126   **b.** 66   **c.** 54

_____

15. What does y represent when $y \div 3$ equals each number? When $4y$ equals each number?

   a. 8   **b.** 20   **c.** 12

_____

Name _____ Date _____

Model Equations

Example   Use the equation $n + 5 = 10$.

- Solve the equation.
- Add 3 to both sides. Solve the new equation.
- Then multiply both sides by 6. Substitute the solution to the original equation in the new equation.

$n = 5$

$n + 8 = 13$ $n = 5$

$6(n + 8) = 78$

$6n + 48 = 78$ $6(5) + 48 = 78$

$\qquad\qquad\qquad 78 = 78$

Use the equation $y + 4 = 7$ for Problems 1-4.

1. Solve the equation. _____

2. Add 7 to both sides. Solve the new equation. _____

3. Then subtract 5 from both sides. Solve the new equation. _____

4. Then multiply both sides by 3. Substitute the solution to the original equation in the new equation. _____

Use the equation $3x = 12$ for Problems 5–8.

5. Solve the equation. _____

6. Multiply both sides by 5. Solve the new equation. _____

7. Then add 6 to both sides. Solve the new equation. _____

8. Subtract 3 from each side. Substitute the solution to the original equation in the new equation. _____

Problem Solving • Reasoning
Use the equation $x = 5$ for Problems 9 and 10.

9. What operation could you perform on both sides to get the new equation $5x = 25$?

10. What operations could you perform on both sides to get the new equation $(5x) + 11 = 36$?

_____   _____

Name _____ Date _____

Functions and Variables

Find the value of y when x = 2.

Example

$y = 3x$
$y = 3 \times 2$
y = 6

1. $y = x + 13$

_____

2. $y = (20x) + 2$

_____

3. $y = 7x - 10$

_____

4. $y = (3x) + 1$

_____

5. $y = 2 + (9x)$

_____

6. $y = (x + 14) \div 4$

_____

7. $y = 23 - 5x$

_____

8. $y = (12 \div x) + 8$

_____

Write an equation for each function.

9. y is equal to the product of x and 10. _____

10. y is equal to 1 less than 3 times x. _____

Describe each function in words.

11. $t = (2m) + 2$

12. $v = 4w$

13. $p = (3m) - 6$

_____

_____

Problem Solving • Reasoning

14. Bill earns $7 for each hour he works. From each paycheck, $10 is deducted for health insurance. How much is Bill's paycheck if he works 32 hours? 40 hours?

15. There are 8 servings in a bag of popcorn. How many bags of popcorn are needed to serve x number of people? 24 people?

_____

_____

Name _____   Date _____

Problem Solving Application: Use Equations

Solve.

1. Steven ran 4 times as far at the track meet as Marco did. If Steven ran 5.2 miles, how far did Marco run?

> **Think:** Do I multiply or divide to solve this problem?

_____

2. At the high-jump event, Maria jumped 2 times as high as Carla. If Maria jumped 66 inches, how high did Carla jump?

> **Think:** Was Carla's jump higher or lower than Maria's jump?

_____

3. The refreshment stand sold $15.76 worth of juice during the track meet. This was $5.60 less than 3 times the amount they made from candy sales. How much did they make from candy sales?

_____

4. There are 48 members on the track team and 4 coaches. The head coach ordered 100 T-shirts. If each coach received 1 T-shirt and the others were divided among the track team members, how many T-shirts did each track member receive?

_____

Choose a Strategy.

Solve. Use these or other strategies.

Problem-Solving Strategies			
• Guess and Check	• Use a Table	• Find a Pattern	• Write an Equation

5. The track team has a fund-raiser each year to buy uniforms. They raised $120 the first year, $240 the second year and $480 the third year. If this pattern continues, how much money could they expect to raise the fourth year?

_____

6. If a bottle of water costs $0.89 at the concession stand, how many bottles could Mike buy with $10.00? How much change would he receive?

_____

Name _____   Date _____

Customary Units of Length

Use a ruler. Measure each line segment to the nearest inch,
half inch, quarter inch, and eighth inch.

Example 
The segment is
3 inches long when measured to the nearest inch,
3 inches long when measured to the nearest half inch,
$2\frac{3}{4}$ inches long when measured to the nearest quarter inch
and $2\frac{7}{8}$ inches long when measured to the nearest eighth inch.

1. •————————————————•

_____

2. •————————————————•

_____

3. •————————————————•

_____

4. •————————————————————•

_____

5. •————————————————•

_____

Problem Solving • Reasoning

6. Draw a line segment that is
$2\frac{1}{8}$ inches long.

_____

7. Give a length that would be 4 inches
when measured to the nearest inch,
and $3\frac{3}{4}$ inches when measured to the
nearest quarter inch.

_____

Name _____ Date _____

Perimeter and Area in Customary Units

Complete.

Example

9 ft = _____ in.
Since 1 ft = 12 in.,
multiply 9 by 12.
9 × 12 = 108
9 ft = **108 in.**

1. _____ in. = 4 yd

2. _____ in. = 8 ft

3. 3 mi = _____ ft

4. 24 yd = _____ ft

5. _____ in. = 3 ft 4 in.

6. _____ ft = 4 yd 2 ft

7. 8,000 ft = _____ mi _____ ft

8. 114 in. = _____ ft _____ in.

Find the perimeter and area of each rectangle.

9.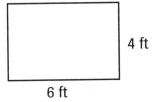
4 ft
6 ft

10.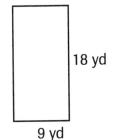
18 yd
9 yd

11.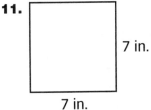
7 in.
7 in.

_____   _____   _____

Problem Solving • Reasoning

12. How much more area does a square with side length 3 inches have than a square with side length 2 inches?

_____

13. Sally needs 150 square inches of material for a project. The material comes in rolls 12 inches wide. If she buys a section 12 inches long, will she have enough material? Explain.

_____

Name _____   Date _____

Customary Units of Weight and Capacity

Complete.

Example

4 T = _____ lb
Since 1 T = 2,000 lb,
multiply 4 by 2,000.
4 × 2,000 = 8,000
4 T = 8,000 lb

1. _____ lb = 208 oz

2. 22,000 lb = _____ T

3. 6 T = _____ lb

4. _____ lb = 96 oz

5. _____ oz = 9 lb

6. 72 oz = _____ lb _____ oz

7. 13,200 lb = _____ T _____ lb

8. 14 c = _____ pt

9. _____ pt = 12 qt

10. 6 pt = _____ c

Algebra • Expressions

Simplify each expression given a = 6 oz, b = 7 lb, and c = 2 lb 8 oz.

11. $a + b$ _____

12. $b + c$ _____

13. $c - a$ _____

14. $(b - c) + a$ _____

Problem Solving • Reasoning

15. Jennifer needs 100 ounces of apple juice to make punch for her birthday party. How many quarts does she need to buy?

_____

16. Paul is making trail mix using 26 ounces of peanuts, 14 ounces of dried bananas, 8 ounces of dried apricots, 12 ounces of dried oranges, and 20 ounces of pretzels. How many pounds will the trail mix weigh altogether?

_____

Name _____   Date _____

Problem-Solving Skill: Solve Multistep Problems

Solve. Use the information from the table to help you.

Gretchen's Garden Shop			
Geraniums	$1.39	Pansies	$.88
Impatiens	$.34	Daisies	$.74
Roses	$14.00	Violets	$1.06

1. Jimmy has $30.00. Does he have enough money to buy 6 geraniums and 24 violets? Explain.

Think: How much would the flowers cost?

_____

2. Would 24 daisies or 48 impatiens be more expensive? What is the difference in price?

Think: What do I need to know difference in price?

_____

3. How much change from a $50.00 bill would be received after buying a dozen violets and 10 geraniums?

_____

4. How much more do 13 pansies cost than 13 daisies?

_____

Choose a Strategy

Solve. Use these or other strategies.

Problem-Solving Strategies

• Find a Pattern   • Make a Table   • Write an Equation   • Work Backward

5. Impatiens also come in packages of 24 for $7.50. If you buy a package of 24 instead of 24 separate impatiens, how much would you save?

_____

6. Geraniums are supposed to be planted 6 inches apart. If you plant 4 geraniums in a row, what is the distance between the plants on the ends?

_____

Name _____ Date _____

Metric Units of Length

Use a ruler to measure each line segment to the nearest decimeter, centimeter, and millimeter.

1. •————————————————————————•

   _____

2. •——————————————————————————————•

   _____

3. •———————————————————•

   _____

4. •——————————————————————•

   _____

Complete each equivalent measure.

5. 4 m = _____ cm

6. _____ dm = 7 m

7. 2,100 cm = _____ m

8. 340 dm = _____ cm

9. 4 km = _____ m

10. 12,000 m = _____ km

Problem Solving • Reasoning

11. What are the length and width of this worksheet to the nearest centimeter?

    _____

12. Give a length in millimeters that would be 1 dm to the nearest decimeter, and 14 cm to the nearest cm.

    _____

Name _____ Date _____

Metric Units of Mass and Capacity

Complete.

> **Example**
>
> 5 kg = ___ g
> Since 1 kg = 1,000 g,
> multiply 5 by 1,000.
> 5 × 1,000 = 5,000
> 5 kg = **5,000 g**

1. 8 L = ___ ml

_____

2. 5,000 g = ___ kg

_____

3. 6 t = ___ kg

_____

4. 3 L 48 ml = ___ ml

_____

5. 23 g = ___ mg

_____

6. 9,000 kg = ___ t

_____

7. 42,000 mg = ___ g

_____

8. 4 kg 300 g = ___ g

_____

Compare. Write >, <, or =.

9. 4 kg ◯ 400 g

10. 4,000 mL ◯ 3 L

11. 800 g ◯ 8 kg

12. 14 kg ◯ 15,000 g

13. 7,000 mL ◯ 7 L

14. 9,000 mL ◯ 90 L

15. 3,000 kg ◯ 3 t

16. 20 L ◯ 3,000 mL

17. 6,000 kg ◯ 60 t

Problem Solving • Reasoning

18. One pound is about 2,200 grams. About how many kilograms are in 10 pounds?

_____

19. Walter received a package with a mass of 2 kg 430 g. What is the mass of the package in grams?

_____

Name _____ Date _____

Add and Subtract Units of Time

How many hours and minutes are there between these times?

Example

1:07 P.M. to 6:20 P.M.
  6 h 20 min
−1 h 7 min
  5 hours 13 minutes

1. 12:58 A.M. to 3:58 A.M.
_____

2. 8:21 P.M. to 11:53 P.M.
_____

3. 2:46 P.M. to 4:14 P.M.
_____

4. 4:52 P.M. to 11:21 P.M.
_____

5. 9:55 A.M. to 1:57 P.M.
_____

6. 3:49 P.M. to 3:43 A.M.
_____

7. 7:47 A.M. to 8:46 P.M.
_____

8. 2:18 A.M. to 8:44 A.M.
_____

9. 4:36 A.M. to 6:13 A.M.
_____

Algebra • Equations
Find the time represented by *t*.

10. $6:15 - t = 1$ h 5 min
_____

11. $t - 1:55 = 2$ h 10 min
_____

12. $3:45 - t = 3$ h 30 min
_____

13. $t - 8:20 = 2$ h 15 min
_____

Problem Solving • Reasoning

14. Henry arrived at the swimming pool at 11:30 A.M. If he stayed until 3:15 P.M., how long did he stay at the pool?
_____

15. Jacob started raking leaves at 1:42 P.M. If he finished at 3:04 P.M., how long did he rake leaves?
_____

Name _____ Date _____

Problem-Solving Strategy: Make a Table

Solve.

1. Joshua swims laps at the pool. On three consecutive weeks, he swam 10 laps, 12 laps, and 14 laps. If this pattern continues, how many laps will he swim in the fourth and fifth weeks?

   Think: What pattern can you find in the increasing numbers?

   _____

2. The first week, Joshua could swim a lap in 84 seconds. The second week he could swim a lap in 80 seconds. The third and fourth weeks he could do it in 77 seconds and 75 seconds. If this pattern continues, how long will it take him to swim a lap the fifth week?

   Think: What pattern can you find in the decreasing numbers?

   _____

3. Josh could hold his breath for 19 seconds the first week. Each week, he was able to hold his breath 8 seconds longer than the week before. In what week was Josh able to hold his breath more than one minute?

   _____

4. The water temperature averaged 75° the first week and rose 1.5° each week until reaching 87°. It then increased 1° each week until reaching 90°. In what week did the water temperature reach 90°?

   _____

Choose a Strategy

Solve. Use these or other strategies.

Problem-Solving Strategies			
• Make a Table	• Work Backward	• Guess and Check	• Write an Equation

5. A bag holds 57 green and blue marbles. There are 13 more blue marbles than green marbles. How many marbles of each color are there?

   _____

6. The temperature at 7:00 P.M. was 72°F. The temperatures at 8:00 P.M., 9:00 P.M. and 10:00 P.M. were 70°F, 68°F, and 66°F. If the pattern continues, when will the temperature be 60°F?

   _____

Name _____ Date _____

Integers and Absolute Value

Example ⁻4
⁻4 is four units from zero, so the absolute value of ⁻4 is **4**.

Write the absolute value of each integer.

1. ⁻6   **2.** ⁻1   **3.** ⁻6   **4.** ⁺10

_____ _____ _____ _____

5. ⁻5   **6.** ⁺13   **7.** ⁺17   **8.** ⁻12   **9.** ⁺14

_____ _____ _____ _____ _____

10. ⁺24   **11.** ⁻51   **12.** ⁻67   **13.** ⁺44   **14.** ⁻31

_____ _____ _____ _____ _____

15. ⁻21   **16.** ⁺27   **17.** ⁻43   **18.** ⁺52   **19.** ⁻69

_____ _____ _____ _____ _____

20. ⁻63   **21.** ⁻70   **22.** ⁺26   **23.** ⁺61   **24.** ⁻57

_____ _____ _____ _____ _____

25. ⁺100   **26.** ⁻148   **27.** ⁺134   **28.** ⁻162   **29.** ⁺192

_____ _____ _____ _____ _____

Problem Solving • Reasoning

30. The temperature at midnight at the North Pole was ⁻4°F. At noon the temperature was 2°F. How much did the temperature change?

_____

31. How many numbers have an absolute value of 12? What are they?

_____

Name _____ Date _____

Use Models to Add Integers

Write the addition expression shown by the counters and then find the answer. White counters represent positive numbers. Black counters represent negative numbers.

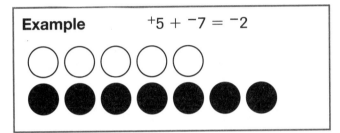

Example $^+5 + {}^-7 = {}^-2$

1.

_____

2.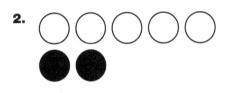

_____

3.

_____

Use two-color counters to find each sum.

4. $^+7 + {}^-4$ _____

5. $^+3 + {}^+4$ _____

6. $^-4 + {}^+2$ _____

7. $^+5 + {}^-7$ _____

8. $^-3 + {}^-5$ _____

9. $^+4 + {}^-8$ _____

Problem Solving • Reasoning

Negative integers are used in golf scoring. The less your score, the better.

10. On the first hole of golf, Mr. Bentfeld scored $^-2$. On the next hole he scored $^-1$. Add the scores from the first two holes to find his score so far.

_____

11. On the last three holes, Mr. Bentfeld scored $^-2$, $^+3$, and $^-2$. Add the scores to find his score for the three holes.

_____

Practice 5-11

Name _____ Date _____

Add Integers on a Number Line

Use the number line to add.

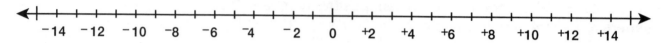

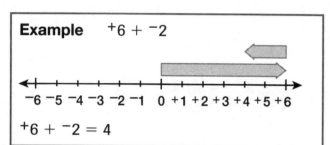

Example $^+6 + {}^-2$

$^+6 + {}^-2 = 4$

1. $^-2 + {}^+5$ _____

2. $^-8 + {}^+10$ _____

3. $^-6 + {}^-3$ _____

4. $^+8 + {}^+6$ _____

5. $^-8 + {}^+7$ _____

6. $^-1 + {}^-9$ _____

7. $^+11 + {}^-9$ _____

8. $^-10 + {}^+7$ _____

9. $^+7 + {}^-19$ _____

10. $^-11 + {}^+10$ _____

11. $^-7 + {}^+16$ _____

12. $^-8 + {}^+12$ _____

13. $^+13 + {}^-1$ _____

14. $^+3 + {}^-12$ _____

Algebra • Equations

Solve for x. Use a number line to help you.

15. $^-15 + x = {}^-13$ _____

16. $x + {}^-5 = {}^+3$ _____

17. $^+6 + x = {}^-3$ _____

18. $x + {}^+7 = {}^-7$ _____

Problem Solving • Reasoning

19. In a game, Patricia scored 3 points and then lost 7 points. What is her score so far?

20. Carl won 6 points, lost 5 points, won 2 points, and lost 4 points. How many points does he need to win to have zero points?

60 Use with text pages 218–219.

Name _____ Date _____

Use Models to Subtract

Use two-color counters to find each difference.

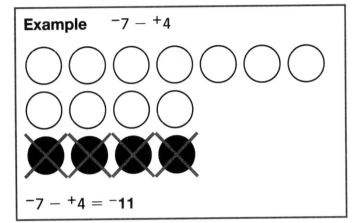

Example $^-7 - {}^+4$

$^-7 - {}^+4 = {}^-11$

1. $^+3 - {}^+4$

_____

2. $^-2 - {}^+6$

_____

3. $^+5 - {}^-7$

_____

4. $^-5 - {}^-8$

_____

5. $^+4 - {}^-8$

_____

6. $^-2 - {}^-4$

_____

7. $^+3 - {}^+5$

_____

8. $^-5 - {}^+12$

_____

9. $^+8 - {}^+5$

_____

Problem Solving • Reasoning

10. Fred has $^-3$ points and then loses another 5 points. Write a subtraction expression that shows his score. Solve the expression to find his score.

_____

11. Find $^+3 - {}^-4$ and $^-4 - {}^+3$. Do you get the same answer? Explain.

_____

Name _____ Date _____

Subtract Integers on a Number Line

Complete each pair of number sentences.

> **Example** $^-3 - {}^-4 = {}^+1$
>
> $^-3 + {}^+4 = {}^+1$
>
>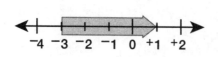
> $^-4 \quad {}^-3 \quad {}^-2 \quad {}^-1 \quad 0 \quad {}^+1 \quad {}^+2$

1. $^-5 - {}^-2 =$

$^-5 + {}^+2 =$

_____

2. $^+6 - {}^-4 =$

$^+6 + {}^+4 =$

_____

3. $^-5 - {}^+3 =$

$^-5 + {}^-3 =$

_____

4. $^-7 - {}^-4 =$

$^-7 + {}^+4 =$

_____

5. $^+10 - {}^+8 =$

$^+10 + {}^-8 =$

_____

6. $^-8 - {}^-12 =$

$^-8 + {}^+12 =$

_____

7. $^+8 - {}^-2 =$

$^+8 + {}^+2 =$

_____

8. $^-9 - {}^+8 =$

$^-9 + {}^-8 =$

_____

Problem Solving • Reasoning

9. Richard has $15 and loans $11 to Gary. Write an addition expression that would represent the amount of money Richard has. Write a subtraction expression that would represent the amount of money Richard has.

_____

10. Randy borrowed $17 from Wendy. Later, he gave her $9 back. Write a subtraction expression that represents the amount of money that Randy owes Wendy. Find the amount that Randy still owes by solving the expression.

_____

Name _____ Date _____

Add and Subtract Integers

Example
$^-3+{}^-4={}^-7$

Decide if each sum or difference will be positive or negative. Then add or subtract.

1. $^+9+{}^-8$ _____

2. $^-4-{}^+9$ _____

3. $^-2+{}^+4$ _____

4. $^+1+{}^-10$ _____

5. $^+5+{}^-1$ _____

6. $^-6+{}^+3$ _____

7. $^-7-{}^-8$ _____

8. $^-10+{}^+1$ _____

9. $^+4+{}^-10$ _____

10. $^-9-{}^-6$ _____

11. $^-10-{}^+2$ _____

12. $^-4+{}^-8$ _____

13. $^+8-{}^-2$ _____

14. $^-6-{}^+5$ _____

15. $^-10+{}^+8$ _____

16. $^+12-{}^+3$ _____

17. $^-9+{}^-2$ _____

18. $^+7+{}^-3$ _____

19. $^+5+{}^-10$ _____

Problem Solving • Reasoning

20. Becky has $12 saved. Her mother loans her enough money so that she can buy an item that costs $19. How much does Becky owe her mother?

_____

21. Larry owes Paul $7. Then he borrows $9 more. How much does Larry owe?

_____

Name _____ Date _____

Problem-Solving Application: Use Integers

Solve.

1. Ingrid borrowed $7. Then she paid back
$4. Then she borrowed $6 more. How
much does she owe now?

> **Think:** How do I represent borrowing
> and returning money?

_____

2. The set of integers (⁻2, ⁺5, ⁻1, 0)
represents the number of yards earned
on 4 plays of a game. Did the team gain
or lose yards altogether?

> **Think:** How does 0 affect the sum of
> the first 3 integers?

_____

3. Marilyn had 12 marbles in her hand. She
put 3 in her marble jar, then removed 7
from the jar, then put 5 in the jar. How
many marbles does she now have?

_____

4. The set of integers (⁺5, ⁻2, ⁺9) represents
the movement of a mail clerk up and
down the floors of a skyscraper. What
increase or decrease in floor height is
represented by the set of integers?

_____

Choose a Strategy

Solve. Use these or other strategies.

Problem-Solving Strategies

• Find a Pattern	• Draw a Diagram	• Use Logical Thinking

5. In four turns, Daniel scored ⁻2, ⁺5, ⁻6,
and ⁺2 points. Did he gain or lose points
on these four turns? How many points?

_____

6. The temperature fell 9°. The current
temperature is ⁻4°F. What was the
original temperature?

_____

7. Study this sequence of integers.
        ⁻7, ⁻10, ⁻13, ⁻16, ⁻19
What is the next integer in the sequence
likely to be?

_____

8. Sandra walked forward 4 steps,
backward 9 steps, and forward 3 steps.
Is she ahead or behind where she
started? How many steps?

_____

Name _____   Date _____

Stem-and-Leaf Plots

The fifth-grade class went on a bird-watching trip. Each group kept track of the number of birds they observed. The data was displayed in a stem-and-leaf plot.

Use the stem-and-leaf plot to answer the questions.

Number of Birds Observed by Each Group	
stem	leaf
0	2, 4
1	2, 5, 6, 9
2	2, 3, 5, 7, 9, 9, 9
3	1, 3, 3

1. What does 1| mean?

_____

_____

3. How many groups observed fewer than 10 birds?

_____

5. How many groups are there?

_____

2. Which stem has four leaves? List them.

_____

4. What number occurs most often? How many times does it occur?

_____

6. Make a stem-and-leaf plot for this set of data: 12, 38, 26, 8, 9, 14, 27, 25, 11, 4, 24, 36

_____

Problem Solving • Reasoning

7. What does it mean if a number occurs more than once in a row of a stem-and-leaf plot?

_____

_____

8. A set of data has numbers from 3 to 56. How many stems will there be if a stem-and-leaf plot is made?

_____

Name _____   Date _____

Double Bar Graphs

The Pet Club took a survey of the fifth- and sixth-graders. Use the graph to answer the questions.

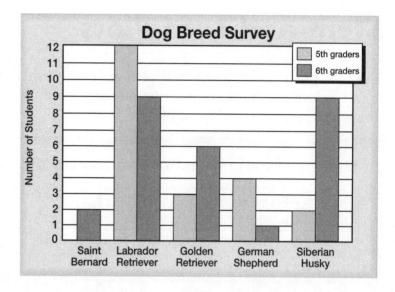

Example

How many more sixth-graders than fifth-graders have golden retrievers?

$6 - 3 = 3$

1. How many students have Saint Bernards?

_____

2. For what breed of dog is there the largest difference between the numbers of fifth- and sixth-graders who own that type of dog?

_____

3. What is the most popular breed of dog?

_____

4. What breeds have a difference of 3 between the fifth- and sixth-graders?

_____

5. How many students own the least popular type of dog?

_____

Problem Solving • Reasoning

Use the graph to answer Problems 6-7.

6. For which breed of cat is there the smallest difference?

_____

7. Can you tell how many students were surveyed? Explain.

_____

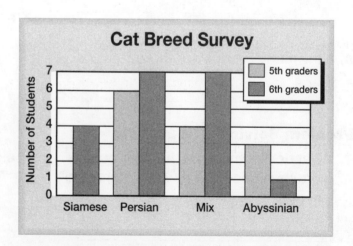

Name _____ Date _____

Histograms

Use the histogram to answer the questions.

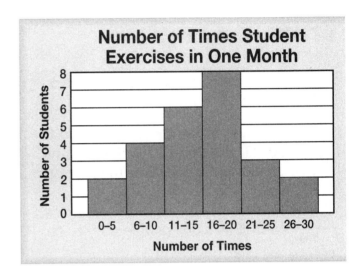

Number of Times Student Exercises in One Month

Example
How many more students exercise 11–15 times per month than exercise 26–30 times per month?   6 – 2 = 4

1. What intervals contain the same number of students?

_____

2. How many students exercise at least 16 times per month?

_____

3. Do more students exercise 15 or fewer times per month or 16 or more times per month?

_____

_____

4. Which interval has the greatest number of students? The fewest?

_____

_____

Problem Solving • Reasoning

5. Make a frequency table and histogram for the data below.

Number of Sports Played

5, 1, 3, 3, 2, 6, 0, 4, 8, 6, 7, 3, 4, 4, 5, 1, 5, 1,
1, 2, 3, 7, 5, 4, 3, 0, 3, 4

_____

6. How many students were surveyed?

_____

Name _____   Date _____

Problem-Solving Skill: Choose Information From a Graph

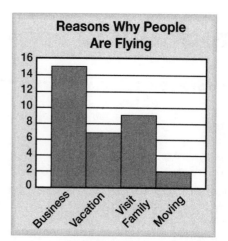

Reasons Why People Are Flying

Use information from the graphs to solve each problem.

1. A survey was taken at O'Hare airport in Chicago. The graph shows the reasons why people are flying. How many people were surveyed?

 Think: How many people does each bar represent?

_____

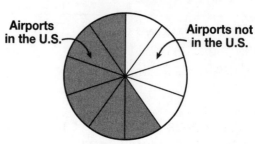

Airports in the U.S.   Airports not in the U.S.

2. The circle graph shows the location of the 10 busiest airports in the world. What fraction of these airports are in the U.S.?

 Think: How many equal sectors are there on the circle graph?

_____

3. How many people were flying because of business?

_____

4. What fraction of the world's 10 busiest airports are not in the U.S.?

_____

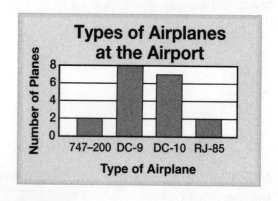

Types of Airplanes at the Airport

Number of Planes

747–200   DC-9   DC-10   RJ-85

Type of Airplane

Choose a Strategy

Solve. Use these or other strategies.

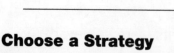 **Problem-Solving Strategies**

| • Guess check | • Work Backwards | • Draw a Diagram | • Use a Graph |

5. What types of planes are in equal number?

6. How many airplanes are at the airport altogether?

Name _____   Date _____

Interpret Line Graphs

Use graph to answer the questions.

Example
What does point A represent?
<u>the beginning of the hike</u>

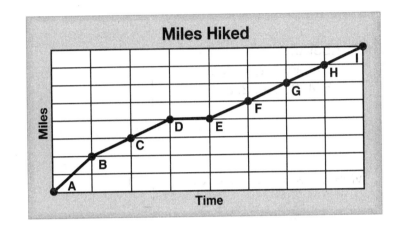

1. Between what two consecutive points did they hike the greatest distance?

_____

2. What happened between points D and E?

_____

3. On what intervals was their speed the same as it was between B and C?

_____

4. When was their speed greater: between A and B or between E and F?

_____

5. Is time on the graph most likely measured in hours, minutes, or seconds? Explain.

_____

_____

Problem Solving • Reasoning

6. A line graph shows the distance from home on a bicycle ride. What does it mean when the graph rises? When the graph falls?

_____

_____

_____

7. A line graph shows the distance from home on a bicycle ride. What would the graph look like at a time when the riders stopped for lunch?

_____

_____

_____

Name _____ Date _____

Line and Double Line Graphs

Shelby kept track of refreshment sales at the school fair. Use the graphs to answer the questions.

1. During which intervals did the refreshment stand make the most money?

_____

2. During which intervals did the refreshment stand make the least money?

_____

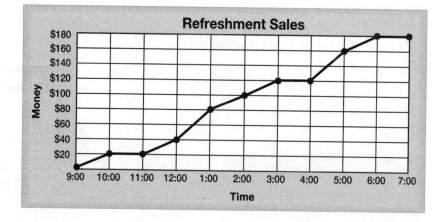

3. Which sold more, orange juice or apple juice?

_____

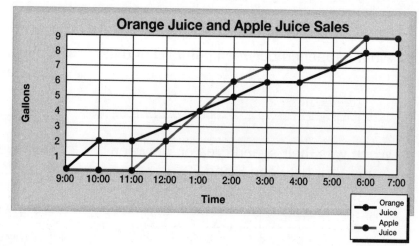

Problem Solving • Reasoning

4. Why are the lines for orange juice and apple juice different? Explain.

_____

_____

5. At what times were orange juice and apple juice sales equal?

_____

Name _____ Date _____

Choose an Appropriate Graph

Choose and make an appropriate graph for the data given.

Example

Masses of Objects in Men's Olympic Throwing Events

Event	Mass
Javelin	0.8 kg
Discus	2.0 kg
Shot Put	7.26 kg
Hammer	7.26 kg

____bar graph____

1. Student 100 m Sprint Times

Time	Number of Students
10–12 sec	3
13–15 sec	5
16–18 sec	10
19–21 sec	6
22–24 sec	2

2. Current Olympic Throwing Event Records

Event	Record
Javelin, women's	74.68 m
Javelin, men's	89.66 m
Discus, women's	72.30 m
Discus, men's	68.82 m
Shotput, women's	22.41 m
Shotput, men's	22.47 m

3. Students' Favorite Sports

Sport	Number of Students
Baseball	16
Football	8
Soccer	12
Softball	4
Hockey	4
Tennis	44

Problem Solving • Reasoning

4. What kind of data is best represented by a bar graph?

5. If you wanted to make a pictograph for the data set in Problem 3, how many students should each picture represent? Explain.

Name _____   Date _____

Problem-Solving Strategy: Make a Table

Use the table below to solve each problem.

Top Agricultural Producers			
Product	**Top Producer**	**Second**	**Third**
Corn	US	China	Brazil
Potatoes	Russia	Poland	China
Rice	China	India	Indonesia
Soybeans	US	Brazil	China
Coffee	Brazil	Columbia	Indonesia
Tea	India	China	Sri Lanka
Rubber	Malaysia	Indonesia	Thailand

source: The Dorling Kindersley Visual Encyclopedia, 1995

1. What countries appear in all three categories?

Think: What information will I start with?

_____

2. What country appears most in the table?

Think: How can I organize the information?

_____

3. List the countries that appear more than two times in the table.

_____

4. List the country that appears twice as a top producer.

_____

Choose a Strategy

Solve. Use these or other strategies.

Problem-Solving Strategies

• Make a Table	• Use Logical Thinking	• Guess and Check	• Write an Equation

5. Use a line plot to find the number of countries that only appear once in the table.

_____

6. Find the average number of letters in the names of the products in the table.

_____

Name _____ Date _____

Make Choices

Make an organized list to show all possible outcomes.

Example

Snack Choices	
Vegetables	**Fruits:**
carrot	banana
celery	apple
cucumber	

carrot/banana, carrot/apple,
celery/banana, celery/apple,
cucumber/banana, cucumber/apple

1.

Report Topics	
Math	**Geography**
Graphs	United States
Measurement	Canada
	Mexico

_____

_____

_____

2.

Framing Choices	
Mat	**Frame**
green	oak
red	gold
white	painted

_____

_____

_____

_____

3.

Furniture Styles	
Chair	**Ottoman**
Plaid	with
Floral	without
Solid	

_____

_____

_____

_____

Multiply to find the number of possible combinations if you can make one choice from each category.

4. 4 dresses, 6 sizes

_____

5. 3 meats, 5 cheeses

_____

Problem Solving • Reasoning

6. David is making a menu poster for school. He can choose from 4 different designs and 3 different sizes. How many possible combinations are there?

_____

7. Madison can choose from 5 different main dishes and 3 different deserts. How many possible meal combinations are there?

_____

Name _____ Date _____

Probability

Use the spinner for Problems 1–7. Tell whether each event is equally likely, likely, unlikely, certain, or impossible.

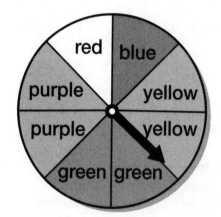

Example
red
_____ **unlikely** _____

1. blue

_____

2. red or blue

_____

3. orange

_____

4. yellow or blue

_____

5. blue, yellow, red, green, or purple

_____

6. yellow or purple

_____

7. red or yellow

_____

Problem Solving • Reasoning

Suppose a coin is tossed 2 times. The possible outcomes are heads/heads, heads/tails, tails/heads, and tails/tails.

8. Is it equally likely, very likely, unlikely, certain, or impossible that the same face shows both tosses?

_____

9. Is it equally likely, very likely, unlikely, certain, or impossible that the tosses are heads/tails?

_____

Name _____ Date _____

Find Probability

Use the shapes to answer the problems. If the shapes
are placed in the bag, picked without looking, and then put back,
what is the probability of each event?

Example

a white square

$\dfrac{\text{number of white squares}}{} = \dfrac{2}{16} = \dfrac{1}{8}$

1. a black triangle

_____

2. a triangle

_____

3. a dotted shape

_____

4. a square

_____

5. a white triangle

_____

6. any triangle or a black circle

_____

7. not a white square

_____

8. a black or white circle

_____

Problem Solving • Reasoning

9. Name an event that has a probability of $\dfrac{1}{16}$.

_____

_____

10. Name an event that has a probability of $\dfrac{7}{16}$.

_____

_____

Name _____ Date _____

Problem-Solving Application: Use Data

Use data to make predictions about outcomes.
Use the table to answer 1–3.

1. On which bus is it more likely to find a girl?

_____

Number of People on the Bus		
	Bus A	Bus B
Girls	22	8
Boys	15	23

2. If you choose a person at random from Bus B, what is the probability that the person is a boy?

_____

3. If you choose a person at random from Bus A, what is the probability that the person is not a boy?

_____

Choose a Strategy

Solve. Use these or other strategies.

Problem-Solving Strategies

• Draw a Diagram	• Write an Equation	• Make a Table	• Guess and Check

4. Suppose you toss 3 coins. What is the probability that all 3 coins show heads?

_____

5. What is the mean of the numbers on a number cube that is labeled 1 to 6?

_____

6. Suppose you roll a number cube that is labeled 1 to 6 twice and add the numbers together. What sum is most likely?

_____

7. A spinner is divided into 8 equal sections. If the spinner lands on red, Player A wins. If it lands on blue, Player B wins. If it lands on green, neither wins. Describe a way to color the spinner so the game is fair.

_____

Name _____ Date _____

Simplest Form

Simplify each fraction. If a fraction is already in simplest form,
just write the fraction.

Example

$\frac{6}{9} = \frac{6 \div 3}{9 \div 3} = \frac{2}{3}$

1. $\frac{3}{21}$ _____

2. $\frac{5}{20}$ _____

3. $\frac{12}{15}$ _____

4. $\frac{8}{12}$ _____

5. $\frac{9}{21}$ _____

6. $\frac{15}{35}$ _____

7. $\frac{20}{24}$ _____

8. $\frac{42}{48}$ _____

9. $\frac{16}{20}$ _____

10. $\frac{36}{45}$ _____

11. $\frac{8}{10}$ _____

12. $\frac{10}{20}$ _____

13. $\frac{14}{21}$ _____

14. $\frac{6}{12}$ _____

15. $\frac{22}{32}$ _____

16. $\frac{35}{49}$ _____

17. $\frac{22}{88}$ _____

18. $\frac{26}{28}$ _____

19. $\frac{18}{90}$ _____

Problem Solving • Reasoning

20. The swim team has 40 members. 8 of the members are boys. Write the number of boys on the team as a fraction in simplest form.

21. Write $0.98 as a fraction of a dollar in simplest form.

Name _____ Date _____

Fractions, Decimals, and Mixed Numbers

Compare. Write >, <, or = for each ◯.

Example

2.4 ◯ $2\frac{3}{5}$

2.4 ◯ 2.6

2.4 < 2.6

2.4 < $2\frac{3}{5}$

1. $\frac{2}{5}$ ◯ $\frac{3}{5}$

2. 2.5 ◯ $2\frac{1}{6}$

3. $\frac{7}{10}$ ◯ 0.07

4. 0.6 ◯ $\frac{1}{5}$

5. 9.08 ◯ $9\frac{1}{5}$

6. $2\frac{1}{4}$ ◯ $2\frac{4}{5}$

7. $\frac{1}{4}$ ◯ $\frac{1}{5}$

Order each set of numbers from least to greatest.

8. $\frac{1}{2}$, $\frac{6}{10}$, 0.2, 0.4

9. $\frac{3}{10}$, 0.75, 1.2, $1\frac{1}{10}$

10. 3.6, 3.55, 1.8, $\frac{2}{10}$

_____

_____

_____

Problem Solving • Reasoning

11. Pete counted that $\frac{4}{10}$ of the students bought lunch at the cafeteria on Monday. On Tuesday 0.75 of the students bought lunch. On which day did more students buy lunch?

12. The Jones's garden covered $1\frac{2}{10}$ acres of land this year. Next year they are planning a garden that is 1.25 acres. Which year will the Jones's garden be larger, this year or next?

_____

_____

Name _____   Date _____

Compare Fractions

Compare these numbers. Write >, <, or = for each $\bigcirc$.

Example

$$\frac{5}{7} \bigcirc \frac{2}{9}$$

$$\frac{5 \times 9}{7 \times 9} \bigcirc \frac{2 \times 7}{9 \times 7}$$

$$\frac{45}{63} > \frac{14}{63}$$

$$\frac{5}{7} > \frac{2}{9}$$

1. $\frac{9}{10} \bigcirc \frac{3}{5}$

2. $\frac{1}{8} \bigcirc \frac{1}{6}$

3. $\frac{5}{7} \bigcirc \frac{7}{10}$

4. $\frac{2}{3} \bigcirc 3$

5. $\frac{9}{8} \bigcirc 1\frac{1}{8}$

6. $\frac{1}{3} \bigcirc \frac{2}{5}$

7. $3\frac{2}{5} \bigcirc \frac{19}{6}$

8. $\frac{17}{12} \bigcirc \frac{19}{10}$

9. $\frac{19}{7} \bigcirc 2\frac{7}{9}$

10. $\frac{7}{12} \bigcirc \frac{5}{7}$

11. $5\frac{2}{3} \bigcirc \frac{27}{5}$

Problem Solving • Reasoning

12. Jan averaged the amount of miles she jogged in two weeks. The mean was $2\frac{3}{5}$ miles and the mode was $2\frac{3}{4}$ miles. Which is greater?

13. Order the numbers and find the median and mode.

$0, 1\frac{1}{10}, 1\frac{2}{5}, 1\frac{2}{5}, \frac{2}{5}, \frac{3}{10}, \frac{3}{5}$

_____

_____

Name _____ Date _____

Problem-Solving Skill: Is the Answer Reasonable?

Tell whether each statement is reasonable or unreasonable. Explain your answer.

1. Jan is running 1 lap, or $\frac{1}{4}$ of a mile, in the track competition. She came in first place. It took her 5 hours to finish.

> **Think:** How long does it take to walk a lap around the track?

_____

2. Steve met his friend at the beach. Steve drove 55 mph and his friend drove 60 mph. Steve's friend could drive farther than Steve in the same amount of time.

> **Think:** How fast do they drive?

_____

3. Steve's family paid $67.99 for a hotel room on their trip. They paid with a $100.00 bill. They received $33.01 change.

_____

4. Jim and his family were at the beach in Florida for 7 days. He was in the sun for 140 hours.

_____

Choose a Strategy

Tell if each statement is reasonable or unreasonable and why you think so. Use these or other strategies.

Problem-Solving Strategies

• Guess and Check	• Work Backward	•Use Logical Thinking

5. Steve spent about as much on Souvenirs as he did on Snacks and Museum Tickets combined.

_____

_____

6. Steve spent the most on snacks.

_____

Steve's Vacation Expenses	
Souvenirs	$27.82
Snacks	$23.45
Museum Tickets	$4.95

Name _____   Date _____

Add and Subtract Fractions with Like Denominators

Add or subtract. Show each answer in simplest form.

Example

$$\frac{3}{7} + \frac{2}{7} = \frac{3+2}{7} = \frac{5}{7}$$

1. $\frac{3}{9} + \frac{5}{9} =$

_____

2. $\frac{8}{9} - \frac{1}{9} =$

_____

3. $\begin{array}{r} \frac{2}{8} \\ +\frac{1}{8} \\ \hline \end{array}$

4. $\begin{array}{r} \frac{5}{10} \\ -\frac{2}{10} \\ \hline \end{array}$

5. $\begin{array}{r} \frac{7}{12} \\ -\frac{5}{12} \\ \hline \end{array}$

6. $\begin{array}{r} \frac{8}{11} \\ +\frac{5}{11} \\ \hline \end{array}$

7. $\frac{4}{5} + \frac{3}{5}$

_____

8. $\frac{9}{15} - \frac{2}{15}$

_____

9. $\frac{5}{12} + \frac{7}{12}$

_____

10. $\frac{2}{3} - \frac{1}{3}$

_____

11. $\frac{15}{16} - \frac{3}{16}$

_____

12. $\frac{7}{8} + \frac{7}{8}$

_____

Problem Solving • Reasoning

13. There are 12 students in art class. 5 students are sketching, 3 students are painting, and the rest are coloring. What fraction of the art students are sketching or painting?

_____

14. Max swam $\frac{1}{4}$ of a mile on Monday and $\frac{2}{4}$ of a mile on Tuesday. How far did he swim on Monday and Tuesday?

_____

Name _____   Date _____

Add Fractions With Unlike Denominators

Add. Write each sum in simplest form.

Example

$$\frac{3}{8} \longrightarrow \frac{18}{48}$$
$$+\frac{1}{6} \longrightarrow +\frac{8}{48}$$

$$\frac{18}{48} + \frac{8}{48} = \frac{26}{48}$$

$$\frac{26}{48} = \frac{2 \times 13}{2 \times 24} = \frac{13}{24}$$

1.
$$\frac{3}{7}$$
$$+\frac{1}{21}$$

2.
$$\frac{1}{15}$$
$$+\frac{2}{3}$$

3. $\frac{7}{8} + \frac{1}{4}$

4. $\frac{1}{4} + \frac{5}{6}$

5. $\frac{1}{6} + \frac{5}{9}$

_____

_____

_____

6. $\frac{4}{5} + \frac{2}{3}$

7. $\frac{2}{15} + \frac{1}{6}$

8. $\frac{7}{9} + \frac{2}{3}$

_____

_____

_____

Problem Solving • Reasoning

9. On Wednesday Jim's bean plant was $\frac{1}{2}$ of an inch tall. On Monday, the bean plant was $\frac{5}{6}$ of an inch taller. How tall was the bean plant on Monday?

10. Michelle ate $\frac{1}{6}$ of the pizza and Charles ate $\frac{7}{12}$ of his. How much pizza did they eat altogether?

_____

_____

Name _____   Date _____

Use the LCD to Add Fractions

Write the LCM of each number pair.

Example
8, 6
8 = **2** × 2 × 2
6 = **2** × 3
LCM = 2 × 2 × 2 × 3
LCM = **24**

1. 12, 18

_____

2. 3, 7

_____

3. 9, 18

_____

Add. Write each sum in simplest form.

4. $\dfrac{5}{9}$
       $+\dfrac{7}{12}$

5. $\dfrac{5}{16}$
       $+\dfrac{3}{4}$

6. $\dfrac{7}{10}$
       $+\dfrac{5}{12}$

7. $\dfrac{1}{2} + \dfrac{1}{3}$

_____

8. $\dfrac{2}{10} + \dfrac{3}{15}$

_____

9. $\dfrac{2}{9} + \dfrac{5}{6}$

_____

Problem Solving • Reasoning

10. Laura bought a granola bar for $0.80. What fraction of a dollar did she spend?

_____

11. Dan completed $\dfrac{2}{3}$ of his homework assignment in class. He finished $\dfrac{1}{4}$ more in the library. How much did he complete altogether?

_____

Name _____ Date _____

Add Mixed Numbers

Write the LCM of each number pair.

Example
12, 15
$12 = 2 \times 2 \times \mathbf{3}$
$15 = \mathbf{3} \times 5$
LCM $= 2 \times 2 \times 3 \times 5$
LCM $= \mathbf{60}$

1. 5, 9

_____

2. 6, 9

_____

3. 3, 6

_____

Write each mixed number in simplest form.

4. $2\frac{5}{15}$

_____

5. $6\frac{4}{18}$

_____

6. $2\frac{12}{15}$

_____

Add. Write each sum in simplest form.

7. $3\frac{1}{10}$
$+1\frac{7}{12}$

8. $5\frac{5}{8}$
$+2\frac{3}{4}$

9. $1\frac{3}{4} + 2\frac{1}{3}$

_____

Problem Solving • Reasoning

10. Ken measured $3\frac{2}{3}$ feet tall last year. This year he grew $1\frac{1}{2}$ feet. How tall is he?

_____

11. Dan drove $1\frac{1}{4}$ miles to pick up a friend for school and then drove $9\frac{4}{5}$ miles to school. How far did he drive?

_____

Name _____ Date _____

Rename Before You Subtract

Write the missing number.

Example

$$1 = \frac{\blacksquare}{8} = \frac{8}{8}$$

1. $1 = \frac{4}{\blacksquare}$ _____

2. $\blacksquare = \frac{10}{10}$ _____

3. $1 = \frac{\blacksquare}{7}$ _____

Write each difference in simplest form. Check your work.

4. 6
   $-1\frac{2}{3}$

5. $7\frac{3}{5}$
   $-2\frac{4}{5}$

6. $8\frac{1}{16}$
   $-3\frac{7}{16}$

7. $5 - 2\frac{1}{5}$ _____

8. $8\frac{3}{7} - 6\frac{3}{7}$ _____

9. $9\frac{3}{8} - 1\frac{5}{8}$ _____

10. $6 - 4\frac{3}{9}$ _____

11. $7\frac{1}{6} - 2\frac{5}{6}$ _____

12. $5\frac{3}{14} - 2\frac{9}{14}$ _____

Problem Solving • Reasoning

13. Jan has read $5\frac{5}{6}$ books this week. Her goal is to read 8 books by the end of the month. How much more does she need to read to meet her goal?

_____

14. Mike must be 4 feet tall in order to ride the rollercoaster at the park. He is $3\frac{1}{4}$ feet tall. How much taller does he need to be in order to ride the rollercoaster?

_____

Name _____ Date _____

Subtract Fractions with Unlike Denominators

Write the difference in simplest form. Check your work.

Example
$5\frac{5}{6} = \quad 5\frac{5}{6}$
$-1\frac{2}{3} = -1\frac{4}{6}$
$\overline{\qquad\qquad} \quad \overline{4\frac{1}{6}}$
Check: $4\frac{1}{6} + 1\frac{4}{6} = 5\frac{5}{6}$

1.
$$\frac{5}{12}$$
$$-\frac{1}{6}$$
$$\overline{\qquad}$$

2.
$$7\frac{2}{9}$$
$$-3\frac{1}{5}$$
$$\overline{\qquad}$$

3.
$$9\frac{1}{8}$$
$$-3$$
$$\overline{\qquad}$$

4.
$$8\frac{2}{3}$$
$$-6\frac{1}{6}$$
$$\overline{\qquad}$$

5.
$$\frac{8}{15}$$
$$-\frac{1}{5}$$
$$\overline{\qquad}$$

6.
$$2\frac{5}{6}$$
$$-1\frac{1}{8}$$
$$\overline{\qquad}$$

7.
$$\frac{9}{10}$$
$$-\frac{1}{4}$$
$$\overline{\qquad}$$

8.
$$5\frac{1}{2}$$
$$-2\frac{1}{6}$$
$$\overline{\qquad}$$

Problem Solving • Reasoning

9. Emma is hiking a $3\frac{7}{10}$ mile trail. She just came up on the $2\frac{1}{2}$ mile marker. How much farther does she need to hike to finish?

10. Jan is baking muffins. The recipe calls for $3\frac{1}{2}$ cups of flour. She only has $2\frac{1}{4}$ cups. How much more does she need?

_____ _____

Name _____ Date _____

Subtract Mixed Numbers

Write each difference in simplest form. Check your work.

Example

$$5\frac{5}{6} = 5\frac{5}{6}$$
$$-2\frac{1}{3} = -2\frac{2}{6}$$
$$\overline{\qquad} \quad \overline{3\frac{3}{6} = 3\frac{1}{2}}$$

Check: $3\frac{1}{2} + 2\frac{1}{3} =$
$3\frac{3}{6} + 2\frac{2}{6} = 5\frac{5}{6}$

1. $7\frac{1}{8}$
   $-2\frac{3}{6}$

2. $9\frac{1}{6}$
   $-3\frac{5}{7}$

3. $7\frac{1}{5}$
   $-2\frac{1}{8}$

4. $9\frac{2}{3}$
   $-2\frac{1}{2}$

5. $4\frac{1}{4}$
   $-2\frac{5}{6}$

6. $7\frac{15}{16}$
   $-2\frac{4}{8}$

7. $9\frac{1}{8}$
   $-2\frac{1}{3}$

8. $5\frac{4}{5}$
   $-2\frac{1}{4}$

Problem Solving • Reasoning

9. Mark walked $\frac{2}{3}$ of a mile and swam $\frac{3}{4}$ of a mile. Did he walk or swim farther? How much farther?

10. Liz practiced the piano $2\frac{1}{2}$ hours last week and $2\frac{1}{3}$ hours this week. Did she practice more hours this week or last week? How much more?

Name _____   Date _____

Problem-Solving Application: Use Patterns

Solve.

1. Kris is giving her friends oatmeal cookies. For every 5 bags she uses $\frac{1}{5}$ of the cookies she baked. How many bags can be filled from 1 batch of oatmeal cookies?

    Think: How would a chart help solve this problem?

2. Every 2 days Jon drinks $\frac{1}{4}$ of a gallon of milk. How many weeks will it take Jon to drink 1 gallon of milk?

    Think: How could a chart help you solve this problem? How many days are in a week?

Choose a Strategy

Solve. Use these or other strategies.

```
        Problem-Solving Strategies

• Find a Pattern    • Guess and Check    • Use Logical Thinking    • Work Backward
```

3. There are 28 students in science class. One fourth are girls. How many boys are in science class?

4. Mark has run 6 miles of the race. That is $\frac{1}{3}$ of the entire race. How far is the entire race?

5. 24 students in art class are separated into groups of 2 to work on a project. Each group spent $\frac{1}{4}$ of an hour working on the project. How many total hours did the students spend working on the craft?

6. Write the next three possible fractions in the pattern. Explain your answer.

   $$\frac{1}{2} = \frac{2}{4} = \frac{4}{8} = \frac{8}{16}$$

Name _____ Date _____

Model Multiplication of Fractions

Example

$\frac{2}{3} \times \frac{2}{5} = \frac{4}{15}$

Use models to find each product.

1. $\frac{1}{2} \times \frac{2}{3}$ _____

2. $\frac{2}{5} \times \frac{1}{3}$ _____

3. $\frac{1}{3} \times \frac{3}{4}$ _____

4. $\frac{1}{6} \times \frac{2}{3}$ _____

5. $\frac{4}{5} \times \frac{2}{3}$ _____

6. $\frac{4}{5} \times 8$ _____

7. $\frac{1}{2} \times 7$ _____

8. $\frac{9}{5} \times \frac{1}{4}$ _____

9. $\frac{8}{7} \times \frac{3}{4}$ _____

Name _____   Date _____

Multiply Fractions

Example
$\frac{3}{4} \times \frac{2}{3} = \frac{6}{12} = \frac{1}{2}$

Multiply. Write each answer in simplest form.

1. $\frac{2}{5} \times \frac{3}{5}$ _____

2. $\frac{1}{8} \times 3$ _____

3. $\frac{1}{6} \times \frac{2}{3}$ _____

4. $\frac{4}{5} \times \frac{1}{2}$ _____

5. $\frac{7}{8} \times \frac{2}{5}$ _____

6. $\frac{4}{9} \times \frac{3}{7}$ _____

7. $\frac{1}{5} \times \frac{8}{9}$ _____

8. $\frac{1}{7} \times \frac{3}{10}$ _____

9. $\frac{1}{2} \times \frac{13}{15}$ _____

10. $\frac{2}{3} \times \frac{18}{20}$ _____

11. $\frac{3}{8} \times \frac{4}{7}$ _____

12. $\frac{3}{10} \times \frac{2}{5}$ _____

13. $\frac{4}{7} \times \frac{1}{4}$ _____

14. $\frac{6}{9} \times \frac{2}{3}$ _____

15. $\frac{5}{6} \times \frac{1}{6}$ _____

16. $\frac{3}{4} \times \frac{5}{6}$ _____

17. $5 \times \frac{4}{5}$ _____

18. $\frac{8}{9} \times \frac{2}{5}$ _____

19. $\frac{6}{7} \times \frac{7}{8}$ _____

Problem Solving • Reasoning

20. Mary earns extra money baby-sitting. Last week, she baby-sat for 9 hours. If $\frac{2}{3}$ of those hours were on Saturday, how many hours did she baby-sit on Saturday?

_____

21. Lawrence owns 20 balls. $\frac{4}{5}$ of the balls are larger than a baseball, and $\frac{1}{2}$ of those are soccer balls. How many soccer balls does Lawrence own?

_____

Name _____ Date _____

Multiply Fractions and Mixed Numbers

Example
$2\frac{2}{3} \times \frac{2}{5} = \frac{8}{3} \times \frac{2}{5} = \frac{16}{15} = 1\frac{1}{15}$

Write each product in simplest form.

1. $1\frac{1}{5} \times \frac{3}{4}$ _____

2. $\frac{1}{8} \times 3$ _____

3. $3\frac{1}{6} \times \frac{2}{5}$ _____

4. $\frac{4}{5} \times 2\frac{1}{2}$ _____

5. $1\frac{3}{8} \times \frac{1}{5}$ _____

6. $2\frac{4}{5} \times \frac{3}{7}$ _____

7. $3\frac{1}{4} \times \frac{8}{9}$ _____

8. $\frac{4}{7} \times 2\frac{3}{4}$ _____

9. $1\frac{2}{5} \times \frac{1}{4}$ _____

10. $\frac{1}{6} \times 3\frac{1}{3}$ _____

11. $\frac{5}{9} \times 3\frac{2}{3}$ _____

Compare. Write >, <, or = for each $\bigcirc$.

12. $2\frac{2}{3} \times \frac{1}{6} \bigcirc 3\frac{1}{2} \times \frac{1}{4}$

13. $\frac{7}{8} \times 4\frac{1}{6} \bigcirc \frac{3}{11} \times 9\frac{1}{2}$

Problem Solving • Reasoning

14. With her dinner, Susan got a super-size cup holding $2\frac{2}{3}$ cups of milk. She was able to drink $\frac{2}{3}$ of the milk. How much milk did she drink?

_____

15. Walt has a piece of rope which is $10\frac{1}{3}$ ft long. He has to cut it into four equal pieces. How long will each piece be?

_____

Name _____   Date _____

Problem-Solving Skill: Choose the Operation

Attendance at the Fireman's Ball has been declining. Each year, the number attending is $\frac{2}{3}$ of the previous year's attendance and the cost of food is $\frac{3}{4}$ that of the previous year.

Remember:
► Understand
► Plan
► Solve
► Look Back

Solve.

1. In what year will the attendance be less than $\frac{1}{3}$ the original attendance?

   Think: When I know one year's attendance, how do I calculate the next year's attendance?

2. There was $1,200 worth of food the first year. What is the difference between the cost of the food in the 2nd and 3rd years?

   Think: When I know the cost of food for one year, how do I find the cost for the next year?

_____   _____

Choose a Strategy

Solve. Use these or other strategies.

Problem-Solving Strategies

• Guess and Check	• Use Logical Thinking	• Work Backward	• Find a Pattern

3. 1 mile is about equal to $1\frac{3}{5}$ kilometers. How many kilometers long is a 26-mile race?

4. Two numbers have a product of $3\frac{1}{5}$ and a sum of $3\frac{3}{5}$. One of the numbers is a whole number. Find the numbers.

_____   _____

5. Theo's bedroom measures $12\frac{3}{4}$ ft by $9\frac{2}{3}$ ft. What is the difference between the length and width of the room?

6. Theo wants to put a dinosaur border around the perimeter of his room. How many rolls of border must he buy if each one covers 10 ft?

_____   _____

Name _____   Date _____

Divide by a Unit Fraction

Example

$$2 \div \frac{1}{4}$$

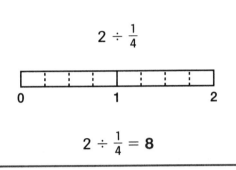

$$2 \div \frac{1}{4} = 8$$

Find each quotient. Check your answers.

1. $3 \div \frac{1}{3}$ _____   2. $5 \div \frac{1}{3}$ _____

3. $6 \div \frac{1}{3}$ _____   4. $1\frac{1}{3} \div \frac{1}{3}$ _____

5. $2\frac{1}{4} \div \frac{1}{4}$ _____   6. $3\frac{1}{2} \div \frac{1}{2}$ _____

7. $5 \div \frac{1}{2}$ _____   8. $3 \div \frac{1}{5}$ _____   9. $1\frac{1}{4} \div \frac{1}{4}$ _____   10. $1\frac{2}{3} \div \frac{1}{3}$ _____

11. $2 \div \frac{1}{5}$ _____   12. $4\frac{1}{3} \div \frac{1}{3}$ _____   13. $2\frac{2}{5} \div \frac{1}{5}$ _____   14. $1\frac{3}{4} \div \frac{1}{4}$ _____

Write the dividend, divisor and quotient that is modeled by each number strip.

15.

_____

16.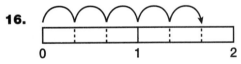

_____

Draw a number strip to model each division.

17. $7 \div \frac{1}{2}$

18. $4\frac{2}{3} \div \frac{1}{3}$

Problem Solving • Reasoning

19. For banana splits, Emily cut 6 bananas each into thirds. How many pieces of banana does Emily have?

20. Abe needs to measure $2\frac{2}{3}$ cups of sugar using a $\frac{1}{3}$ cup measuring cup. How many times should he fill the measuring cup?

_____   _____

Name _____   Date _____

Divide by a Counting Number

Example
$\frac{4}{5} \div 4 = \frac{\cancel{4}^{1}}{5} \times \frac{1}{\cancel{4}_{1}} = \frac{1}{5}$

Divide by multiplying by a unit fraction.

1. $2 \div 3$ _____

2. $5 \div 10$ _____

3. $\frac{4}{7} \div 2$ _____

4. $1\frac{1}{3} \div 3$ _____

5. $2 \div 5$ _____

6. $3\frac{1}{3} \div 2$ _____

7. $\frac{5}{8} \div 5$ _____

8. $\frac{3}{5} \div 4$ _____

9. $\frac{5}{4} \div 2$ _____

10. $\frac{2}{3} \div 4$ _____

11. $2\frac{1}{3} \div 7$ _____

12. $4 \div 3$ _____

13. $\frac{2}{5} \div 3$ _____

14. $1\frac{3}{4} \div 3$ _____

15. $\frac{5}{3} \div 5$ _____

16. $\frac{5}{6} \div 2$ _____

17. $3\frac{1}{2} \div 4$ _____

18. $\frac{7}{5} \div 5$ _____

19. $3\frac{1}{5} \div 4$ _____

20. $4\frac{2}{3} \div 7$ _____

Problem Solving • Reasoning

21. A box of 48 cookies is divided into 6 pouches. How many cookies are in each pouch?

22. A cookie recipe uses $\frac{2}{3}$ cup of brown sugar and makes 24 cookies. How much brown sugar is each in cookie?

_____   _____

Name _____ Date _____

Problem-Solving Strategy: Solve a Simpler Problem

Remember:
► Understand
► Plan
► Solve
► Look Back

Solve each problem, using the Solve a Simpler Problem strategy.

1. On an automobile assembly line, long sheets of metal are cut into pieces $3\frac{4}{5}$ m long for the Racer and $2\frac{5}{8}$ m long for the Speedster. If 10,000 of each car are produced, how much more metal is used in producing the Racers?

Think: How is the difference in the length of the two pieces related to the total difference in the amount of metal used?

2. A certain piece of a car's material expands by $\frac{1}{12}$ its original length in extreme heat. If the piece begins with a length of 30 in., how long will it be after it expands?

Think: How much will the material expand in length? What is the total length after the expansion?

_____

_____

Choose a Strategy

Solve. Use these or other strategies.

Problem-Solving Strategies

| • Guess and Check | • Use a Table | • Work Backward | • Write an Equation |

3. The engineers are divided into groups to work on a project. There are six groups. One-half of the groups have five engineers each, $\frac{1}{3}$ of the groups have six engineers each and $\frac{1}{6}$ of the groups have four engineers each. How many engineers are working on the project?

_____

4. Of the 2,800 cars produced one month, $\frac{1}{14}$ were chosen to be inspected. $\frac{1}{20}$ failed the inspection. How many cars failed inspection?

_____

Name _____   Date _____

Divide by a Fraction

Divide. Write answers in simplest form.

> **Example**
>
> $\frac{2}{3} \div \frac{6}{11} = \frac{2}{3} \times \frac{11}{6} = \frac{22}{18} = \frac{11}{9} = 1\frac{2}{9}$

1. $\frac{2}{3} \div \frac{1}{3}$ _____   **2.** $\frac{1}{3} \div \frac{3}{4}$ _____   **3.** $\frac{5}{8} \div \frac{5}{6}$ _____   **4.** $\frac{3}{5} \div \frac{2}{3}$ _____

5. $\frac{3}{4} \div \frac{2}{3}$ _____   **6.** $\frac{2}{3} \div \frac{4}{7}$ _____   **7.** $\frac{1}{3} \div \frac{7}{10}$ _____   **8.** $\frac{5}{3} \div \frac{1}{3}$ _____

9. $\frac{5}{6} \div \frac{1}{3}$ _____   **10.** $\frac{11}{12} \div \frac{1}{4}$ _____   **11.** $\frac{1}{2} \div \frac{7}{8}$ _____   **12.** $\frac{1}{4} \div \frac{1}{3}$ _____

13. $2\frac{5}{8} \div \frac{1}{8}$ _____   **14.** $\frac{3}{4} \div \frac{3}{8}$ _____   **15.** $1\frac{1}{6} \div \frac{5}{6}$ _____   **16.** $\frac{3}{5} \div \frac{4}{7}$ _____

Problem Solving • Reasoning

17. One-fourth of the students in the fifth grade play baseball. If 30 students play baseball, how many students are in the fifth grade?

18. Marvin is trying to finish a jigsaw puzzle. He has placed $\frac{2}{3}$ of the pieces so far. If he has put in 60 pieces of the puzzle, how many pieces altogether are in the puzzle?

_____   _____

Name _____ Date _____

Divide With Mixed Numbers

Rewrite the expression as a multiplication expression using the reciprocal of the divisor.

Example

$$\frac{2}{3} \div 2\frac{1}{3} = \frac{2}{3} \div \frac{7}{3} = \frac{2}{3} \times \frac{3}{7}$$

1. $\frac{5}{7} \div 2\frac{1}{4}$

2. $\frac{3}{5} \div 4\frac{2}{3}$

_____ _____

3. $\frac{4}{9} \div 1\frac{3}{5}$

4. $\frac{4}{9} \div 5\frac{1}{3}$

5. $1\frac{2}{5} \div 2\frac{3}{4}$

6. $2\frac{3}{8} \div 1\frac{2}{3}$

_____ _____ _____ _____

Write each quotient in simplest form.

7. $\frac{1}{3} \div 2\frac{1}{3}$ _____

8. $\frac{5}{6} \div 1\frac{5}{6}$ _____

9. $\frac{1}{2} \div 3\frac{1}{4}$ _____

10. $1\frac{2}{5} \div 1\frac{3}{5}$ _____

11. $\frac{1}{5} \div 3\frac{4}{5}$ _____

12. $\frac{2}{3} \div 1\frac{1}{9}$ _____

13. $\frac{3}{4} \div 1\frac{1}{2}$ _____

14. $2\frac{1}{3} \div 1\frac{1}{6}$ _____

15. $\frac{7}{8} \div 2\frac{3}{4}$ _____

Problem Solving • Reasoning

16. Taylor collected $4\frac{1}{3}$ gallons of rain water and used $2\frac{1}{2}$ gallons to water her indoor plants. What fraction of the water she collected did she use to water the plants?

17. Zack has a rope $10\frac{1}{2}$ feet long. If he cuts it into pieces each $2\frac{1}{3}$ feet long, how many pieces can he cut?

_____

_____

Name _____   Date _____

Problem-Solving Application: Use Circle Graphs

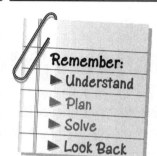

Remember:
► Understand
► Plan
► Solve
► Look Back

Solve. Use the circle graph.

1. If 20 of the fifth graders like to watch football, how many students are in the fifth grade?

> **Think:** Do you need to multiply or divide to solve this problem?

_____

2. What fraction of the students prefer "other" activities?

> **Think:** What is the sum of all the fractions in the circle graph?

_____

Favorite Weekend Activities of 5th Graders

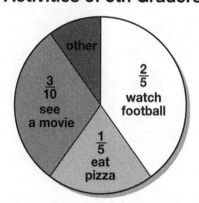

Choose a Strategy

Solve. Use these or other strategies.

Problem-Solving Strategies

• Guess and Check	• Use a Table	• Work Backward	• Write an Equation

3. Which activity is preferred by more than $\frac{1}{3}$ of the fifth graders?

_____

4. One-half of the fifth graders who voted for pizza prefer pepperoni on their pizza. How many students prefer pepperoni pizza?

_____

Name _____ Date _____

Multiply Whole Numbers and Decimals

**Write the number of decimal places you expect in each product.
Then solve.**

Example

1.3
× 3
‾‾‾‾
3.9

There will be one decimal place in the product.

---

1. 5 × 2.2   **2.** 3 × 0.12   **3.** 2.75 × 7   **4.** 1 × 0.124

_____ _____ _____ _____

Multiply.

5. 8 × 0.25   **6.** 2 × 14.1   **7.** 7.6 × 5   **8.** 21.4 × 3

_____ _____ _____ _____

9. 8.2 × 4   **10.** 5 × 2.3   **11.** 3.9 × 9   **12.** 1.57 × 8

_____ _____ _____ _____

Insert a decimal point to make each product correct.

13. 5 × 7.132 = 3566   **14.** 40.689 × 4 = 162756   **15.** 8 × 0.951 = 7608

Problem Solving • Reasoning

16. Red grapes cost $1.19 per pound and green grapes cost $0.92 per pound. Which costs more: 5 pounds of red grapes or 6 pounds of green grapes? How much more?

_____
_____

17. Lamar's Lemonade sells 14 cups of lemonade in one hour. If Lamar charges $0.35 per cup, how much money should be in his cash box?

_____

Name _____ Date _____

Estimate Products

Estimate the products by rounding each factor.

Example
107   rounds to   100
×0.36   ×0.40
40.0

1. 13×0.47

2. 5.96×3

3. 4×2.89

4. 3×3.98

5. 9.87×12

6. 3.075×15

7. 4.46×3

8. 1.52×23

9. 5×3.7

10. 0.124×8

11. $\$4.79 \times 14$

12. $\$2.17 \times 6$

Algebra • Expressions Find a value of n to make each statement true. Multiply to check your estimate.

13. $n \times 15$ is between 20 and 25.

14. $n \times 35$ is between 300 and 310.

Problem Solving • Reasoning

15. Andrea fills her car's 12-gallon tank at the Pump-N-Pay. If gas costs $1.89 per gallon, how much will the fill-up cost?

16. Melissa is renting chairs for a party. Each chair rents for $2.19. How much will it cost Melissa to rent 21 chairs?

Name _____ Date _____

Problem-Solving Strategy: Find a Pattern

Solve each problem, using the Find a Pattern strategy.

1. Lee is planting flowers. If there are 7 flowers in the first row, 13 in the second row, and 19 in the third row, how many are likely to be in the 5th row?

Think: Is there a pattern to how much the number of flowers increases from row to row?

_____

2. Billy's jalepeño pepper plant was 3.7 inches tall when he planted it. After one week, it was 5.1 inches tall; after two weeks, it was 6.5 inches tall. How tall is it likely to be after 4 weeks?

Think: Is there a pattern that you can use to find the plant's height after 4 weeks?

_____

3. Sam starts the week with $30.00. After one day, he has $25.60, after two days, he has $21.20, and after three days he has $16.80. How much is he likely to have after six days?

_____

4. Charlie's goal is to double his savings each month of the year. If he has $30 after one month, how much will he have after seven months?

_____

Choose a Strategy

Solve. Use these and other strategies.

Problem-Solving Strategies			
• **Work Backward**	• **Write an Equation**	• **Make a Table**	• **Find a Pattern**

5. Karyn is packing lunches for her family. She can make either tuna or turkey sandwiches, and can include these side items: chips, carrots, raisins, and apples. How many possible combinations of different sandwiches and side items are possible?

_____

6. To estimate the adult height of a child, you can multiply his height at age 2 by 2. When he was 2 years old, about how tall was a 75-inch tall man?

_____

Name _____ Date _____

Multiply and Divide Decimals by Powers of 10

Multiply or divide by using patterns.

Example

$1.375 \times 10^3 = 1,375$

1. 4.542×10^3 **2.** $3,987 \times 10^2$ **3.** $275 \div 10^1$ **4.** 4.59×10^2

_____   _____   _____   _____

5. 84.39×10^2 **6.** $9,837 \div 10^1$ **7.** $95.37 \div 10^3$ **8.** 0.033×10^2

_____   _____   _____   _____

9. 0.87×10^3 **10.** 945×10^2 **11.** $0.056 \div 10^3$ **12.** $8.577 \div 10^2$

_____   _____   _____   _____

Algebra • Equations Solve for x.

13. $100 = x^2$ **14.** $100,000 = 10^x$ **15.** $1 = 10^x$

_____   _____   _____

Problem Solving • Reasoning

16. A scientist recorded the distance between two stars as 3.45×10^3 miles. In standard form, how far apart are the stars?

17. Marlena paid 100 times as much for her $180,000 house as she did for her computer. How much did she pay for her computer?

_____   _____

Name _____ Date _____

Divide a Decimal by a Whole Number

Find each quotient. Check using multiplication.

Example	$\begin{array}{r} 2.3 \\ 4\overline{)9.2} \\ -8 \\ \hline 1\,2 \\ -1\,2 \\ \hline 0 \end{array}$	Place the decimal point in the quotient directly above the decimal point in the dividend.

1. 27.6 ÷ 3 _____

2. 0.6 ÷ 2 _____

3. $7\overline{)14.7}$

4. $9\overline{)25.2}$

5. $6\overline{)44.4}$

6. 6.58 ÷ 2 _____

7. $5\overline{)8.75}$

8. 3.16 ÷ 4 _____

9. $3\overline{)0.27}$

10. $7\overline{)11.2}$

11. $3\overline{)75.3}$

12. 15.18 ÷ 6 _____

Problem Solving • Reasoning

13. Wendy is splitting $68.96 among four bank accounts. How much money will go into each account?

14. A sailboat travels 24.9 miles in 3 hours. What is its average speed in miles per hour?

_____

_____

Name _____ Date _____

Problem-Solving Skill: Interpret Remainders

Solve.

1. Luke is making flowers out of tissue paper and wire. Each flower requires 3 squares of tissue paper. How many flowers can he make with a package of 25 sheets of tissue paper?

   Think: Can you make part of a flower?

   _____

2. At Bob's Nursery Center, 5 bags of topsoil cost $7.00. How much did each bag cost?

   Think: How many dollars and cents will each ticket cost?

   _____

Choose a Strategy

Solve. Use these and other strategies.

Problem-Solving Strategies

| • Make a Table | • Guess and Check | • Draw a Diagram | • Interpret Remainders |

3. At the pool, Roger swam 18 more laps than Inez. Together, they swam 46 laps. How many laps did Inez swim?

   _____

4. Pedro takes a number, multiplies by 13, then subtracts 20. The result is 97. What was the number?

   _____

5. Fold a page once down the middle, making 2 sections. Fold again down the middle, making 4 sections. How many folds are needed to make 32 sections?

   _____

6. Brian, Charles, Tiffany and Robert are each wearing a different color. They are wearing blue, red, green and white. Charles is not wearing red. A girl is wearing blue. Robert is not wearing red or green. What color is each person wearing?

   _____

Name _____   Date _____

Write Zeros in the Dividend

Divide and check.

Example		Check:		

$$
\begin{array}{r}
15.65 \\
62.6 \div 4 \quad 4\overline{)62.60} \\
-4 \\
\hline
22 \\
-20 \\
\hline
26 \\
-24 \\
\hline
20 \\
-20 \\
\hline
0
\end{array}
$$

Check:
$$
\begin{array}{r}
2\;2\;2 \\
15.65 \\
\times \quad 4 \\
\hline
62.60
\end{array}
$$

1. $3\overline{)57.3}$ **2.** $2\overline{)6.9}$

3. $4\overline{)50}$ **4.** $6\overline{)48.6}$

5. $5\overline{)47}$ **6.** $2\overline{)4.3}$ **7.** $8\overline{)92}$

8. $8\overline{)340}$ **9.** $8.67 \div 4$ _____   **10.** $5.44 \div 5$ _____

11. $8\overline{)42}$ **12.** $18.6 \div 8$ _____   **13.** $8\overline{)56.3}$

Problem Solving • Reasoning

14. Vera is cutting a board 87.4 cm long into 4 equal portions. How long will each portion be?

15. Sarah owns 5 shares of a company's stock. The total value of the shares is $312.82. What is the price of each share?

_____   _____

Name _____   Date _____

Divide by a Decimal

Divide and check.

Example		
$75 \div 0.3$	$\begin{array}{r} 250 \\ 3\overline{)750} \\ -6 \\ \hline 15 \\ -15 \\ \hline 0 \end{array}$	Check: $\begin{array}{r} {\scriptstyle 1} \\ 250 \\ \times\, 0.3 \\ \hline 75.0 \end{array}$

1. $0.5\overline{)45}$

2. $1.2\overline{)48}$

3. $8.2\overline{)82}$

4. $0.4\overline{)32}$

5. $4.5\overline{)27}$

6. $9.5\overline{)114}$

7. $1.4\overline{)280}$

8. $8.5\overline{)340}$

9. $0.8\overline{)17.6}$

10. $2.3\overline{)115}$

11. $7.5\overline{)675}$

Is each quotient reasonable? Check by rounding the divisor to the nearest whole number.

12. $77 \div 5.5 = 1.4$ _____

13. $7 \div 3.5 = 20$ _____

14. $40 \div 0.8 = 50$ _____

Problem Solving • Reasoning

15. Rafi buys 26 raffle tickets for $6.50. What is the cost of each raffle ticket?

_____

16. Pete is 36.18 inches tall. This height is 0.6 times the height of his brother. How tall is Pete's brother?

_____

Name _____ Date _____

Divide a Decimal by a Decimal

Divide. Check each quotient by estimating or by using multiplication.

Example		Check:

$$
2.4\overline{)9.984}
$$

$$
\begin{array}{r}
4.16 \\
24\overline{)99.84} \\
-96 \\
\hline
38 \\
-24 \\
\hline
144 \\
-144 \\
\hline
0
\end{array}
$$

$$
\begin{array}{r}
\overset{1}{\overset{2}{4.16}} \\
\times \quad 24 \\
\hline
1664 \\
8320 \\
\hline
99.84
\end{array}
$$

1. $0.4\overline{)20.8}$ **2.** $0.4\overline{)0.28}$ **3.** $0.5\overline{)4.25}$ **4.** $0.2\overline{)5.6}$

5. $0.06\overline{)0.018}$ **6.** $0.55\overline{)8.8}$ **7.** $7.2\overline{)25.2}$ **8.** $8.3\overline{)26.975}$

Algebra • Equations For each equation, find values for *a* and *b* that make the equation true.

9. $a \div b = 9$ **10.** $a \div b = 6$ **11.** $a \div b = 5$ **12.** $a \div b = 20$

_____   _____   _____   _____

_____   _____   _____   _____

Problem Solving • Reasoning

13. An overseas phone call cost $7.44 for 24.8 minutes. What was the price per minute of the call?

14. One mile is equal to about 1.6 kilometers. About how many miles long is a 5-km race?

_____   _____

Name _____   Date _____

Problem-Solving Application: Use Formulas

Remember:
► Understand
► Plan
► Solve
► Look Back

Solve.

1. The blacktop at Reese elementary is a square whose area is 4,225 square yards. How long is each side of the playground?

    Think: What formula shows how the side length of a square is related to its area?

   _____

2. Part of the blacktop is painted with rectangles of different colors. Each rectangle has a length of 5 feet and a width of 3 feet. What is the perimeter of each rectangle?

   Think: How can you use the side lengths of a rectangle to find its perimeter?

   _____

Choose a Strategy

Solve. Use these and other strategies.

Problem-Solving Strategies

• Guess and Check	• Use Logical Thinking	• Solve a Simpler Problem	• Use Formulas

3. The end zone of the Reese Elementary football field is a rectangle 10 yards long and 160 feet wide. What is its area in square feet?

   _____

4. The school's baseball diamond is a square with sides 90 feet long. How many yards are run by a player scoring 3 home runs?

   _____

5. Mr. Rice brings a bag of 14 balls outside for recess. 8 balls are removed, 3 are replaced, 2 are removed, 4 more are removed, then 6 are replaced. How many balls are in the bag?

   _____

6. Beth, Frank and Tim each play a sport. The names of the players and their sports do not begin with the same letter. The sports are basketball, football and tennis. Frank did not play tennis. A girl did not play football. What sport did Tim play?

   _____

Name _____ Date _____

Points, Lines, and Rays

Describe each pair of lines. If possible, use appropriate symbols to write the relationship.

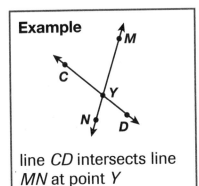

Example

line *CD* intersects line *MN* at point *Y*

1.

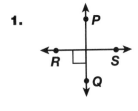

_____

2.

_____

Draw and label a picture for each description.

3. $\overrightarrow{BC}$

4. Point *Q*

5. Plane *XYZ*

6. $\overrightarrow{PR} \parallel \overrightarrow{CJ}$

7. $\overleftrightarrow{RT}$

8. $\overleftrightarrow{KL} \perp \overleftrightarrow{VR}$

9. $\overrightarrow{GH}$

10. $\overline{KH}$

Problem Solving • Reasoning

11. Line *GH* is perpendicular to line *MN*. How many right angles are formed where the two lines intersect?

12. Two parallel lines are crossed by one line that is perpendicular to each of them. How many intersections are there?

_____

_____

Name _____   Date _____

Measure and Draw Angles

Use symbols to name each angle three ways.

Example 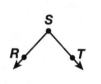 ∠RST; ∠TSR; ∠S	**1.** 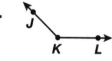 _____ _____ _____	**2.** _____ _____ _____	**3.** _____ _____ _____

Classify each angle as *acute, obtuse, straight* or *right*.

4.	**5.**	**6.**	**7.**
_____	_____	_____	_____

Use a protractor to measure each angle. Write the measure.

8.	**9.**	**10.**
_____	_____	_____

Problem Solving • Reasoning

11. Two sidewalks meet at a 125° angle. Classify this angle as acute, obtuse, right, or straight.

_____

12. The measurement of an acute angle is between ____° and ____°.

_____

Name _____ Date _____

Triangles

Classify each triangle in two ways.

Example

6 cm 6 cm
6 cm

equilateral; acute

1.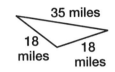

35 miles
18 miles   18 miles

_____
_____

2.

7 in.
9 in.   11.4 in.

_____
_____

3.

6 m
8 m
7 m

_____
_____

Find the missing angle measures.

4.

?
55°

_____

5.

60°
60° ?

_____

6.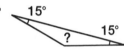

15°
?   15°

_____

7.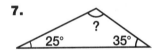

?
25°   35°

_____

Problem Solving • Reasoning

8. Sketch an acute isosceles triangle.

9. Molly says that her right triangle has an obtuse angle. Explain why this is impossible.

_____
_____
_____
_____

Name _____   Date _____

Congruence

Trace each figure. Use a ruler to measure the sides and a
protractor to measure the angles of each figure. Mark and
name the congruent sides and congruent angles.

Example

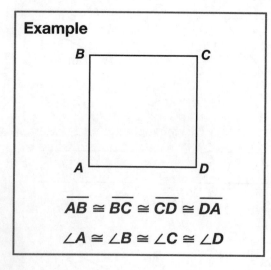

$$\overline{AB} \cong \overline{BC} \cong \overline{CD} \cong \overline{DA}$$

$$\angle A \cong \angle B \cong \angle C \cong \angle D$$

1.

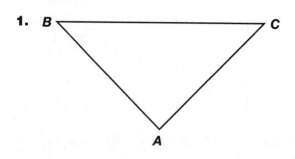

_____

2.

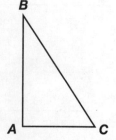

_____

3.

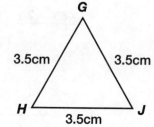

_____

Problem Solving • Reasoning

4. Draw two triangles whose angles
are 45°, 45° and 90° which are not
congruent.

5. If two squares have the same side
lengths, are the two squares necessarily
congruent?

_____

Name _____   Date _____

Quadrilaterals

Classify the figure in as many ways as possible.

Example

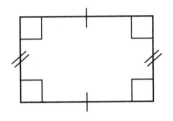

quadrilateral; parallelogram; rectangle

1.

_____

2.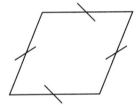

_____

_____

3.

_____

_____

Use the figure to answer each question.

4. Name two congruent triangles.

_____

5. Name a quadrilateral that is not
a parallelogram. _____

6. Name a rectangle. _____

7. Name a trapezoid that is not
a parallelogram. _____

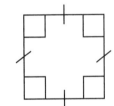

Problem Solving • Reasoning

9. Three of the angles in quadrilateral
ABCD are 40°, 70°, and 100°. What is
the measure of the other angle?

_____

8. Name two triangles which are
not congruent. _____

10. Is every square a rectangle? Explain.

_____

_____

Name _____   Date _____

Problem-Solving Strategy: Solve a Simpler Problem

Solve each problem by solving a simpler problem.

1. How many squares can you find in the figure?

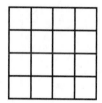

> **Think:** How many sizes of squares can you find in the figure?

_____

_____

_____

2. Josh's little brother made the following design with his building blocks. How many squares can you find in the figure?

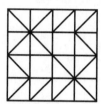

> **Think:** How does the answer to Problem 1 help with this problem?

_____

_____

3. How many squares can you find in the figure?

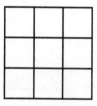

_____

4. How many squares can you find in the figure?

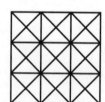

_____

Choose a Strategy

Use these or other strategies to solve.

Problem-Solving Strategies

• Find a Pattern   • Draw a Diagram   • Solve a Simpler Problem   • Guess and Check

5. Josh's brother likes to use multi-colored building blocks to build his towers. If he built a tower with the pattern from the ground up: red, yellow, yellow, blue, what color would the 32nd block be?

_____

6. Josh is paid $2.50 per hour to baby-sit his little brother. If his parents left at 8:30 for a 9:00 meeting that lasted for $1\frac{1}{2}$ hours, and they arrived home $\frac{1}{2}$ hour after the meeting was over, how much would Josh earn baby-sitting?

_____

Name _____   Date _____

Circles and Angles

Use symbols to identify the following parts of this circle.

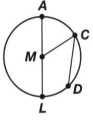

Example
Radii
$\overline{AM}$, $\overline{ML}$, $\overline{MC}$

1. Chords

_____

2. central angles

_____

3. Diameter

_____

Classify each figure as a *radius, diameter, chord* or *central angle*. Indicate if more than one term applies.

4. $\overline{YX}$

_____

5. $\angle YZQ$

_____

6. $\overline{QR}$

_____

7. $\overline{RZ}$

_____

8. $\angle RZX$

_____

9. $\overline{QZ}$

_____

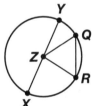

On a separate sheet of paper, construct a circle that contains all of the following:

10. Radius BC

11. Diameter AC

12. Chord MN

Problem Solving • Reasoning

13. Explain the statement:
a radius can never be a chord.

_____

_____

_____

14. If a central angle measures 180°, what is it called?

_____

_____

Name _____ Date _____

Parallel and Perpendicular Lines

Use a compass and a straightedge for Exercises 1–3.

> **Example**
>
> Draw a line labeled *t*. Draw and label a point *S* that is not on line *t*. Construct line *d* that passes through point *S* and is perpendicular to line *t*.
>
>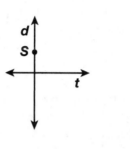

1. Draw and label line *m*. Draw and label a point *Y* that is not on line *m*. Construct line *n* so it passes through point *Y* and is parallel to line *m*.

2. Construct a square and label it *MNOP*.

3. Construct a rectangle and label it *QRST*.

Problem Solving • Reasoning

4. Line *BC* is perpendicular to line *DE*. Line *FG* is perpendicular to line *BC*. What is the relationship between lines *DE* and *FG*?

5. Name two types of quadrilaterals which have two sets of parallel sides.

_____

Name _____ Date _____

Triangles and Rectangles

Complete each construction.

1. Construct triangle *QRS* congruent to equilateral triangle *ABC*.

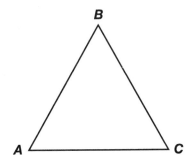

2. Construct rectangle *ABCD* congruent to rectangle *MNOP*.

Problem Solving • Reasoning

3. If square *ABCD* has side length 5 mm, and square *MNPQ* has side length 7 mm, are the two squares congruent? Explain.

4. Are all equilateral triangles congruent? Explain.

_____

_____

Practice 10–10

Name _____ Date _____

Symmetry

Trace each figure and turn it. Then for each figure, write *yes*
or *no* to tell if it has rotational symmetry. If it does, tell how
many degrees you turned it.

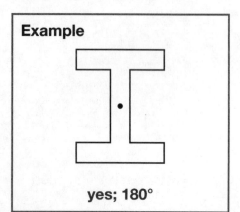

Example

yes; 180°

1.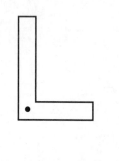

_____

2.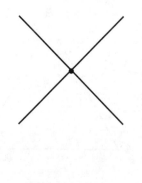

_____

Trace each figure and fold it. Then for each figure, write *yes* or *no*
to tell if it has line symmetry. If it does, write the number of lines
of symmetry that it has.

3.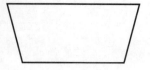

4.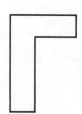

5.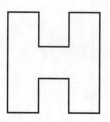

_____ _____ _____

Use a compass, a protractor and another sheet of paper to
draw these figures.

6. A figure with two lines
of symmetry

7. A figure with rotational
symmetry

8. A figure with no lines
of symmetry

Problem Solving • Reasoning

9. Sketch a figure with rotational
symmetry but not line symmetry.

10. How many lines of symmetry does a
square have?

_____ _____

Name _____ Date _____

Problem-Solving Skill: Visual Thinking

Solve.

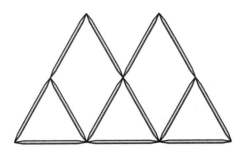

1. Can you remove 5 toothpicks to leave two parallelograms?

> **Think:** How many sides does a parallelogram have?

_____

_____

2. How many toothpicks would you need to remove from the figure to leave three congruent equilateral triangles?

> **Think:** How can you check to see if the figures are congruent?

_____

_____

Choose a Strategy

Solve. Use these or other strategies.

Problem-Solving Strategies			
• Use Logical Thinking	• Draw a Diagram	• Find a Pattern	• Guess and Check

3. The art students used toothpicks to create sculpture. If the students used 40 boxes that contained 1000 toothpicks each and 50 boxes that contained 750 toothpicks each, how many toothpicks did they use?

_____

4. Look at the figure at the top of the page. How could you remove 4 toothpicks to create two equilateral triangles that are NOT congruent?

_____

Name _____   Date _____

Perimeter and Area of Complex Figures

**Find the perimeter and area of each figure.
All intersecting sides meet at right angles.**

Example

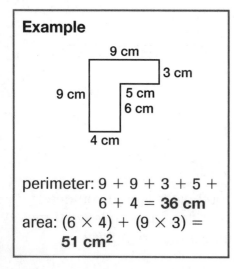

perimeter: 9 + 9 + 3 + 5 +
6 + 4 = **36 cm**
area: (6 × 4) + (9 × 3) =
51 cm²

1.

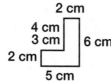

_____

_____

2.

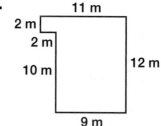

_____

_____

Algebra • Expressions Write an expression to represent the
perimeter of each figure.

3.

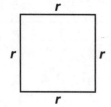

4.

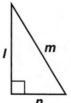

5.

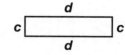

_____   _____   _____

Problem Solving • Reasoning

6. Draw two figures such that the first one
has a greater perimeter but smaller area
than the second.

7. Does it matter which way you divide a
complex figure into simple polygons to
find the area? Use a figure to illustrate
your answer.

_____

_____

Name _____ Date _____

Find the Area of a Parallelogram

Find the area of each figure.

Example 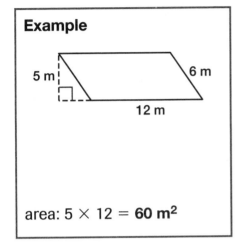 area: 5 × 12 = **60 m²**	**1.** 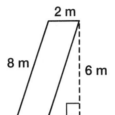 _____

2.
_____

3.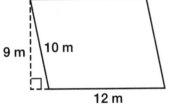

4.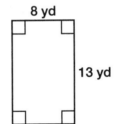

5.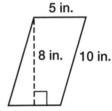

_____ _____ _____

Problem Solving • Reasoning

6. A parallelogram has a base that measures 4 cm and an area of 20 cm². What is the height of the parallelogram?

7. The height of a parallelogram is 1 meter. The area is 2 m². What is the measurement of the base of the parallelogram?

_____ _____

Name _____   Date _____

Find the Area of a Triangle

Find the area of each triangle.

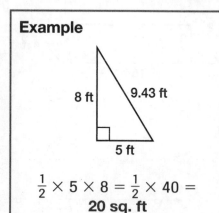

Example

8 ft   9.43 ft

5 ft

$\frac{1}{2} \times 5 \times 8 = \frac{1}{2} \times 40 =$
20 sq. ft

1.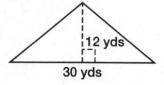
2 m
8 m

_____

2. 9 cm
14 cm

_____

3. 12 yds
30 yds

_____

4.
8 m
4 m

_____

5. 4 ft
10 ft

_____

Algebra • Expressions Write an expression to represent the area of each triangle.

6.
x   z
y

_____

7.
a   c
b

_____

8.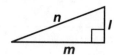
n   l
m

_____

Problem Solving • Reasoning

9. Explain why the area of a triangle is $\frac{1}{2} bh$, while the area rectangle or a parallelogram is expressed as bh.

_____

_____

10. If a right triangle has sides that are 3m, 4m and 5m, what is the area of the triangle?

_____

_____

Name _____ Date _____

Find the Circumference of a Circle

Find the circumference of each circle. Use 3.14 or $\frac{22}{7}$ for π.

Example	1.	2.
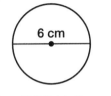 6 cm C = 3.14 × 6 cm = 18.84 cm	5 ft _____	9 m _____

3.	4.	5.
8 ft	10 in.	14 m
_____	_____	_____

Express each circumference as a fraction in simplest form.
Use $\frac{22}{7}$ for π.

6.	7.	8.
$\frac{1}{4}$ m	$2\frac{1}{2}$ ft	$\frac{9}{7}$ yd
_____	_____	_____

Problem Solving • Reasoning

9. If you know the measurement of the radius of a circle, how do you find the circumference?

_____

_____

_____

10. If a circle has a diameter of 1 3/4 ft, what is its circumference?

_____

_____

Name _____   Date _____

Solid Figures

Determine the surface area of each solid figure.

Example

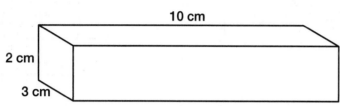

Surface area = 2 × (3 × 2) + 2 × (3 × 10) + 2 × (10 × 2) =
             2 × 6 + 2 × 30 + 2 × 20 =
             12 + 60 + 40 =
             112 cm²

1.

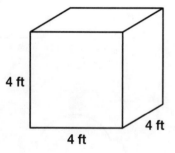

4 ft
4 ft
4 ft

2.

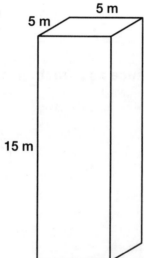

5 m
5 m
15 m

_____   _____

Problem Solving • Reasoning

3. How many flat surfaces make up a rectangular prism?

4. What is the difference between a cube and a rectangular prism?

_____   _____

_____

Name _____ Date _____

Volume

Determine the volume of each solid figure.

Example

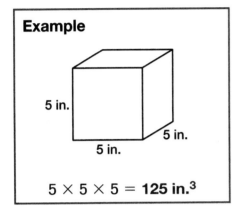

5 in.

5 in.
5 in.

$5 \times 5 \times 5 = 125$ **in.³**

1.
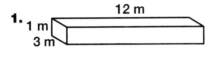
12 m
1 m
3 m

_____

2.
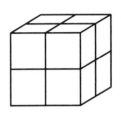

_____

3.
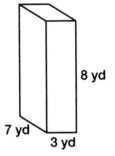
8 yd
7 yd
3 yd

_____

4.
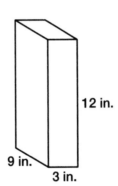
12 in.
9 in.
3 in.

_____

5.
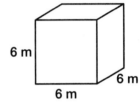
6 m
6 m
6 m

_____

Problem Solving • Reasoning

6. Ron's lunchbox measures 8 in. × 4 in. × 10 in. What is the volume of Ron's lunchbox?

_____

7. Iris' lunchbox has a volume of 300 cubic inches. If its height is 10 in. and its width is 3 in., what is its length?

_____

Name _____   Date _____

Problem-Solving Application: Use Geometry

Solve.

1. Sketch or build a three dimensional figure with these views.

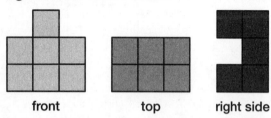

front   top   right side

 Think: Which view tells you what must be in the bottom layer to support the other layers?

2. Sketch the front, top, and right side views of this solid figure.

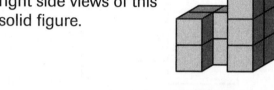

Think: How can you tell if there is a small cube in place if it is hidden from your view?

Choose a Strategy

Use these or other strategies.

Problem-Solving Strategies

• Guess and Check	• Find a Pattern	• Make a Table	• Draw a Diagram

3. What three dimensional figure will this two dimensional shape make when it is folded?

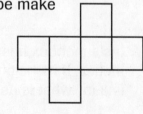

4. When three cubes are lined up side by side, and touching each other, how many of the faces are hidden?

_____

Name _____ Date _____

Meaning of Ratios

A puzzle game has 25 pieces. There are 6 rectangles and 10 triangles. The rest are parallelograms.

Write each ratio three different ways.

Example			
triangles to rectangles	$\frac{5}{3}$	5 to 3	5:3

1. all shapes to triangles

_____

2. parallelograms to all pieces

_____

3. rectangles to parallelograms

_____

4. triangles to parallelograms

_____

5. all shapes to rectangles

_____

6. parallelograms to triangles

_____

7. rectangles to triangles

_____

8. triangles to all shapes

_____

Problem Solving • Reasoning

9. Billy has a bag of shapes. There are 5 squares, 9 triangles, and 7 circles. What is the ratio of circles to squares?

_____

10. Billy sorts the shapes by color. There are 11 blue, 5 yellow, and 5 red shapes. What is the ratio of blue shapes to total shapes?

_____

Name _____   Date _____

Equivalent Ratios

Write two equivalent ratios for each given ratio.

Example
$\frac{2}{5} = \frac{4}{10} = \frac{8}{20}$

1. 3:7

_____

_____

2. 2 to 9

_____

_____

3. $\frac{1}{6}$

_____

_____

4. 2:4

_____

_____

5. 4 to 7

_____

_____

6. $\frac{6}{5}$

_____

_____

7. 5 to 8

_____

_____

Write each ratio as a fraction in simplest form.

8. 16:24

_____

9. 35 to 14

_____

10. 20:15

_____

11. 24:72

_____

Complete each set of equivalent ratios.

12. $\frac{8}{3} = \frac{\blacksquare}{24}$

_____

13. $\frac{6}{21} = \frac{\blacksquare}{7}$

_____

14. $\frac{13}{52} = \frac{1}{\blacksquare}$

_____

Problem Solving • Reasoning

15. Three copies of a book cost $20. Use equivalent ratios to find the cost of nine copies of the book.

_____

16. In a jar, there are nickels and dimes. The ratio of nickels to dimes is 5 to 7. If the jar contains 21 dimes, what is the total number of coins in the box?

_____

Name _____ Date _____

Rates

Find the rate per unit of time.

Example
150 miles in 3 hours
÷ 3   ÷ 3
50 miles per hour

1. 63 yards in 9 minutes   **2.** $2,100 in 4 weeks

_____   _____

3. $135 in 5 hours   **4.** 21 pages in 7 hours   **5.** 642 meters in 6 minutes

_____   _____   _____

Find the distance traveled in the given amount of time.

6. 3 hours at 62 mph   **7.** 12 minutes at 10 m/min   **8.** 6.5 hours at 45 km/h

_____   _____   _____

Find the length of time for each trip.

9. 350 miles at 40 mph   **10.** 150 yards at 2 yd/sec   **11.** 85 km at 17 km/h

_____   _____   _____

Problem Solving • Reasoning

12. Peter runs 3 miles in half an hour. At this rate, how many miles could he run in 2 hours?

13. Chris can assemble a tent in 4 minutes. How many minutes will it take him to assemble 5 tents?

_____   _____

Name _____   Date _____

Scale Drawing

In a scale for a drawing of a road, 1 cm represents 3 m.
The scale is 1 cm:3 m. Find *n* in each case.

Example
7 cm represents *n* m.
n = 21

1. 0.25 cm represents *n* m.
_____

2. *n* cm represents 51 m.
_____

3. 0.5 cm represents *n* m.
_____

4. 5 cm represents *n* m.
_____

5. 1.5 cm represents *n* m.
_____

6. *n* cm represents 1.5 m.
_____

7. *n* cm represents 16.5 m.
_____

8. 4.5 cm represents *n* m.
_____

Find the missing measurements.

Drawing Size	0.25 in.	0.75 in.	1 in.	**11.** _____	1.5 in.	**13.** _____
Actual Size	1 ft	**9.** _____	**10.** _____	5 ft	**12.** _____	9 ft

Problem Solving • Reasoning

14. A map is drawn with a scale of 1 cm:300 km. On the map, the distance between two towns is 12 cm. What is the actual distance between those two towns?

_____

15. A blueprint of a house is made with a scale of $\frac{1}{3}$ in.:2 ft. On the blueprint, a window has a length of 1 inch. How long is the actual window?

_____

Name _____ Date _____

Problem-Solving Skill: Choose a Computation Method

Solve.

1. A map of New York uses a scale of 1 cm:1.2 km. The Verrazano Narrows Bridge is 1.5 cm long on the map. What is the actual length of the bridge?

   Think: What equal ratios can I use to solve this problem?

   _____

2. A map of Florida uses a scale of 1 in.:5 miles. The distance between Lake Worth and Boca Raton is 3 in. on the map. What is the actual distance?

   Think: Can I solve this problem mentally?

   _____

3. A model of an airplane uses the scale of 1 in.:15 ft. If the model's wing is 2.5 inches long, how long is the actual airplane's wing?

4. A scale drawing of a house's second story uses the scale of $\frac{2}{3}$ in.:$2\frac{1}{2}$ ft. If the actual bedroom is $17\frac{1}{2}$ feet long, how long is the bedroom in the drawing?

Choose a Strategy

Solve. Use these or other strategies.

┌─────────────────── **Problem-Solving Strategies** ───────────────────┐
│ • Draw a Diagram • Make a Table • Solve a Simpler Problem • Work Backward │
└──┘

5. On a map, the length of a town is 3.5 cm. The actual length of the town is 7 km. On the map, how many centimeters represent 1 km?

6. On a map, the distance between two stores is 7.5 in. What will this distance become if the map is shrunk so the ratio of the shrunk map to the original map is 1:3?

7. A map has a scale of 1 in.:13 miles. On the map, the distance between the park and the aquarium is 2.5 inches. How far is it from the park to the aquarium?

8. The length of a trail is 72 miles. On a map the trail is 0.8 in. long. How many miles does 1 in. represent on the map?

Name _____   Date _____

Understand Percent

Write each ratio as a percent.

Example
$\frac{87}{100} = 87\%$

1. $\frac{56}{100}$

_____

2. $\frac{29}{100}$

_____

3. $\frac{17}{100}$

_____

4. $\frac{8}{100}$

_____

5. $\frac{38}{100}$

_____

6. $\frac{65}{100}$

_____

7. $\frac{72}{100}$

_____

8. $\frac{9}{100}$

_____

9. 75 parts out of 100

_____

10. 60 parts out of 100

_____

11. 7 parts out of 100

_____

Write each percent as a ratio in simplest form.

12. 44%

_____

13. 62%

_____

14. 80%

_____

15. 77%

_____

16. 4%

_____

17. 19%

_____

Name _____ Date _____

Ratio and Percents

Write each ratio as a percent.

Example
$\frac{29}{50} = \frac{58}{100} = 58\%$

1. $\frac{27}{100}$ _____

2. $\frac{1}{2}$ _____

3. $\frac{3}{4}$ _____

4. $\frac{9}{25}$ _____

5. $\frac{23}{50}$ _____

6. $\frac{41}{50}$ _____

7. $\frac{2}{5}$ _____

Match each percent in column A to an equivalent ratio in column B.

Column A		**Column B**
8. 75%	**a.**	$\frac{3}{10}$
9. 30%	**b.**	$\frac{11}{20}$
10. 55%	**c.**	$\frac{3}{4}$
11. 5%	**d.**	$\frac{1}{20}$

Write each percent as a ratio in simplest form.

12. 44% _____

13. 65% _____

14. 84% _____

15. 15% _____

16. 33% _____

17. 75% _____

18. 72% _____

19. 81% _____

Problem Solving • Reasoning

20. Tony made 85% of his shots in a basketball game. If he took 40 shots, how many shots did he make?

_____

21. There are 25 students in French class. Twelve of them are girls. What percent of the students are boys?

_____

Name _____   Date _____

Decimals and Percents

Write each percent in decimal form and each decimal in percent form.

Example
$4\% = \dfrac{4}{100} = 0.04$

1. 0.33

2. 7%

3. 0.13

_____

4. 0.62

5. 29%

6. 0.99

7. 0.08

_____

8. 15%

9. 25%

10. 0.45

11. 0.72

_____

How many units in a 10-by-10 grid should be shaded to represent each percent or decimal?

12. 21%

13. 0.66

14. 59%

15. 0.45

_____

16. 0.2

17. 18%

18. 43%

19. 0.03

_____

Problem Solving • Reasoning

Use the graph to answer problems 20–21.

A bread recipe contains water, salt, yeast and wheat flour in the percentages shown on the graph.

20. Write a decimal that represents the percent of the recipe that is wheat.

_____

21. What percent of the recipe are salt and water together?

_____

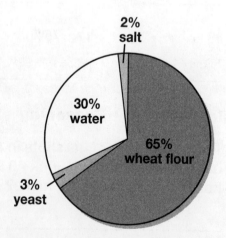

2% salt

30% water

65% wheat flour

3% yeast

Name _____   Date _____

Use Fractions, Decimals, and Percents for Comparisons

Which represents the least part of a unit?

Example
$\frac{7}{10}$ 0.63 47%
$\frac{70}{100}$ $\frac{63}{100}$ $\frac{47}{100}$
$\frac{47}{100}$ is the least

1. 0.11   19% $\frac{1}{10}$

_____

2. 73% $\frac{3}{4}$ 0.69

_____

3. 55% $\frac{1}{2}$ 0.52

_____

4. 0.42 $\frac{2}{5}$ 41%

_____

5. 69% $\frac{7}{10}$ 0.68

_____

Order each set from the greatest to the least parts of a unit.

6. 76% $\frac{37}{50}$ 0.8

_____

7. 0.85 $\frac{8}{10}$ 82%

_____

8. $\frac{14}{25}$ 51%   0.5

_____

9. 0.31   23% $\frac{1}{4}$

_____

10. $\frac{9}{20}$ 58%   0.53

_____

11. 0.68 $\frac{31}{50}$ 60%

_____

Problem Solving • Reasoning

12. Apples and pears were sold at a fruit stand. Two-fifths of the sales were apples and 45% were pears. Which fruit represented a greater portion of the total sales?

_____

13. Forty percent of the students in Mrs. Wong's art class are 9 years old. Another 0.45 are 10 years old, and the rest of the students are 11 years old. What fraction of the students are 11 years old?

_____

Name _____   Date _____

Problem-Solving Strategy: Choose a Strategy

Solve. Choose the best strategy.

1. At McConnor Park, a vendor sells lemonade in two sizes. A 12-oz drink costs $1.55 and a 16-oz drink costs $2.25. Which size offers the better unit price per ounce? Round to the nearest cent.

Think: How can I find the price per ounce of lemonade in each size?

_____

2. About 35% of the people who come to the park bring a pet. $\frac{2}{5}$ of those who come to the park do so to exercise. Which group of people represents a larger percent of the people coming to the park?

Think: How can I compare 35% to the fraction $\frac{2}{5}$?

_____

Choose a Strategy

Solve. Use these or other strategies.

Problem-Solving Strategies

• Draw a Diagram	• Guess and Check	• Find a Pattern	• Work Backward

3. Roger walked his dog 4 times longer than Blake did. Together, they spent 1 hour and 20 minutes walking their dogs. For how long did Roger walk his dog?

_____

4. Sarah pays for an ice-cream cone with 10 coins. She has one more quarter than dime and two more nickels than quarters. The cone cost $1.20. What coins did Sarah use?

_____
_____

Name _____ Date _____

Mental Math: Find 10% of a Number

Find 10% of each number. Use mental math.

Example
$78 \times \frac{1}{10} \longrightarrow 7.8$

1. 4

_____

2. 0.08

_____

3. 327

_____

4. 518.23

_____

5. 19.35

_____

6. 6.23

_____

7. 3,509

_____

Find 20% of each number.

8. 30

_____

9. 200

_____

10. 10

_____

11. 65.5

_____

12. 1.5

_____

13. 423

_____

14. 46

_____

15. 2,046

_____

Problem Solving • Reasoning

16. There are 60 books on a shelf. 10% of them are history books, 30% are biology books and the rest are chemistry books. How many chemistry books are on the shelf?

_____

17. Tom had $5.50 in his pocket. He spent 20% of that amount. How much money does Tom have left?

_____

Name _____   Date _____

Percent of a Number

Solve by writing the percent as a fraction.

Example
Find 20% of 85.
$\frac{20}{100} \times 85 = \frac{1}{5} \times \frac{85}{1} = \frac{85}{5} = 17$

1. 45% of 320   **2.** 50% of 47

_____   _____

3. 30% of 200   **4.** 85% of 150   **5.** 20% of 310   **6.** 50% of 82

_____   _____   _____   _____

Solve by writing the percent as a decimal.

7. 29% of 33   **8.** 18% of 300   **9.** 75% of 21   **10.** 40% of 60

_____   _____   _____   _____

Solve using equal ratios.

11. 60% of 70   **12.** 85% of 80   **13.** 55% of 70   **14.** 35% of 20

_____   _____   _____   _____

Problem Solving • Reasoning

15. The original price of a bike was $248. The bike was on sale for 20% off. If Mike bought the bike on sale, how much did he pay for the bike?

16. A toy car sells for $13.50. How much tax will be charged if the sales tax is 6% of the price?

_____   _____

Name _____ Date _____

Compare Data Sets

Compare. Use >, < or = for each ◯.

<table>
<tr><td>

Example

7 out of 42 ◯ 5 out of 15

$\frac{7}{42}$ ◯ $\frac{5}{15}$

$\frac{1}{6} < \frac{1}{3}$

</td></tr>
</table>

1. 2 out of 10 ◯ 3 out of 9

2. 50 out of 75 ◯ 2 out of 3

3. 4 out of 24 ◯ 5 out of 40

4. 12 out of 60 ◯ 10 out of 40

5. 5 out of 19 ◯ 5 out of 21

6. $\frac{3}{8}$ ◯ $\frac{3}{10}$

7. $\frac{5}{12}$ ◯ $\frac{5}{11}$

8. $\frac{2}{5}$ ◯ $\frac{2}{7}$

9. $\frac{4}{10}$ ◯ $\frac{4}{11}$

10. $\frac{5}{6}$ ◯ $\frac{5}{7}$

11. $\frac{10}{13}$ ◯ $\frac{10}{20}$

Use the illustration to complete Problems 12–13.

12. What percent of the pencils have polka dots?

_____

13. What percent of the gray, black, and white pencils are gray?

_____

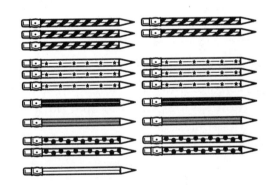

Algebra • Equations

Find each value of n.

14. 10 out of 28 = n out of 56 _____

15. n out of 55 = 7 out of 11 _____

Problem Solving • Reasoning

16. Tina has 400 stickers and Jan has 300 stickers. If 25% of each girl's collection is heart stickers, how many heart stickers does each girl have?

_____

17. Tina has 140 smiley face stickers and Jan has 120. Who has the greater percentage of smiley face stickers? What is the percentage?

_____

Name _____   Date _____

Problem-Solving Application: Use Percent

Solve.

1. A quadrilateral has one angle measuring 138° and two angles each measuring 75°. What percent of the total number of angles does the fourth angle represent?

   Think: What should be the sum of the four angles?

   _____

2. On Tuesday, Bob spent his day doing the following activities:

   Sleeping: 9 hours   Eating: 2 hours
   School: 6 hours   Other: 7 hours

   What percent of his day did Bob spend at school?

   Think: How many hours make up the whole day?

   _____

Choose a Strategy

Solve. Use these or other strategies.

> **Problem-Solving Strategies**
>
> • Use Fractions   • Use Percent   • Use Money/Decimals   • Use Measurement

3. Arnold paid $45.00 to join a health club for one month. If he used the club 11 times, what was the cost per use to the nearest cent?

   _____

4. During the season, a volleyball team's ratio of games won to games lost was 3:2. What percent of their games did they win?

   _____

5. Chuck's little sister is learning to read. She can recognize 17 letters. To the nearest whole number, what percent of the letters in the alphabet can she recognize?

   _____

6. George and Carol both wrote reports for science class. George's report was 408 words long, and was 80% of the length of Carol's report. How long was Carol's report?

   _____

Name _____ Date _____

Transformations

In each pair, the figures are congruent. Tell whether the transformation shown is a translation, reflection, or rotation.

Example

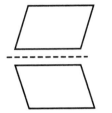

The figure has been flipped over the line, so it is a reflection.

1.

_____

2.

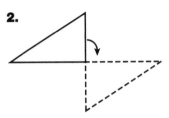

_____

Complete the given transformation.

3. reflection

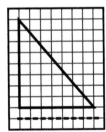

4. rotation

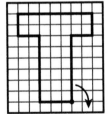

5. translation

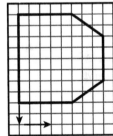

Problem Solving • Reasoning

6. Which type of transformation could be described as a flip?

_____

7. What happens when you translate a figure down three units, then up three units?

_____

_____

_____

Name _____   Date _____

Integers and the Coordinate Plane

Write the ordered pair for each point.

Example
H
To locate point H, travel 3 units right, and down 2 units.
H is located at ($^+$3, $^-$2)

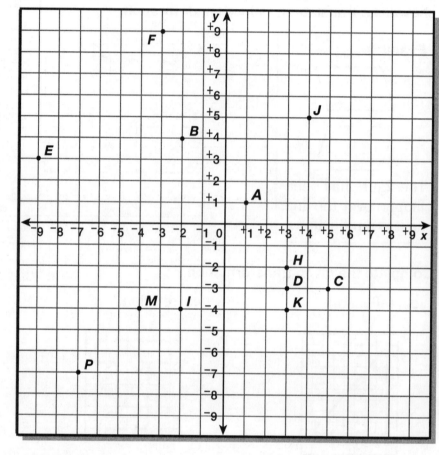

1. I _____

2. A _____

3. C _____

4. B _____

5. D _____

Write the letter name of the point at each location.

6. ($^-$9, $^+$3) _____

7. ($^+$4, $^+$5) _____

8. ($^+$3, $^-$4) _____

9. ($^-$4, $^-$4) _____

10. ($^-$7, $^-$7) _____

11. ($^-$3, $^+$9) _____

Algebra • Expression Use $x = 4$ and $y = 1$ to find the coordinate of each point.

12. $(x + 1, y - 1)$ _____

13. $(x - 3, y + 5)$ _____

14. $(x - 4, y - 1)$ _____

Problem Solving • Reasoning

15. If you drew the points ($^-$3, $^-$3); ($^-$3, $^+$3); ($^+$3, $^+$3) and ($^+$3, $^-$3), and connected the points in that order, what shape would you draw?

_____

16. What kind of triangle is drawn by connecting the points ($^-$2, 0), ($^+$2, 0), and (0, $^+$10)?

_____

Name _____   Date _____

Transformations in the Coordinate Plane

Use the diagram to name the coordinates of triangle *ABC* after each transformation.

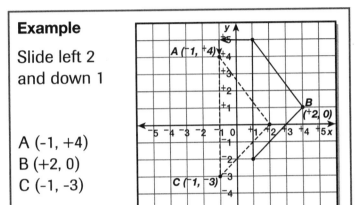

Example

Slide left 2
and down 1

A (-1, +4)
B (+2, 0)
C (-1, -3)

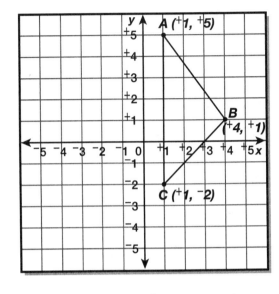

1. Flip over the *y*-axis

_____

2. One half turn about (0,0)

_____

3. Slide right 1 and down 2

_____

4. Slide left 3 and up 1

_____

5. Flip over the *x*-axis.

_____

Find the result of each transformation.

6. Slide the point (+3, ⁻2) left 4 and
up 3.

_____

7. Slide the point (+2, ⁻2) up four units,
then rotate a half turn about (0, 0).

_____

Problem Solving • Reasoning

8. If a point is located at (⁻1, ⁻1) and it
shifts up 1 and to the right 1, where is
it now located?

_____

9. If a point is located at (⁻5, ⁻1) and it
shifts up 1, where is it now located?

_____

Name _____ Date _____

Problem-Solving Strategy: Draw a Diagram

Draw a diagram to solve each problem.

1. How many ways will a regular hexagonal-shaped piece fit into a congruent hole?

Think: Did I try flipping the hexagon and turning it to check all possibilities?

_____

2. How many ways will a right scalene triangle-shaped piece fit in a congruent hole?

Think: Did I try flipping the triangle and turning it to check all possibilities?

_____

3. How many different ways will a rectangular-shaped piece fit into a congruent hole?

_____

4. How many ways will a regular octagon-shaped piece fit into a congruent hole?

_____

Choose a Strategy

Solve. Use these or other strategies.

Problem-Solving Strategies

| • Draw a Diagram | • Guess and Check | • Work Backward | • Find a Pattern |

5. If you know the number of sides of a regular polygon, does that give you a hint as to how many ways it will fit in a congruent shaped hole? Look for a pattern to answer this problem.

_____

6. Tom has a shape that can fit into a congruent shaped hole in six different ways. What is one specific shape that Tom might have?

_____

7. At a burger restaurant, John can choose from beef, turkey or veggie burgers. He can choose whole-wheat, white, or 7-grain buns. How many different burger-bun combinations are possible?

_____

8. Ed lives in a city in which the streets which run north-south are numbered from 1 to 70 from the south and the streets which run east-west are lettered A through W from the west. If Ed starts at the intersection of 4th and E streets and goes 6 blocks north and 8 blocks east, where will he be?

_____

Name _____ Date _____

Integers and Functions

Complete each function table or find the function.

Example

Function: $y = x - 1$

x	y
0	-1
1	0
2	1
-2	-3

$y = 0 - 1 = ^-1 \quad y = ^-1$
$y = 1 - 1 = 0 \quad y = 0$
$y = 2 - 1 = 1 \quad y = 1$
$y = ^-2 - 1 = ^-3 \quad y = ^-3$

1. Function: $y = x + 4$

x	y
-3	
-2	
-1	
0	

2. $y = x + 5$

x	y
5	
4	
-4	
-2	

3. $y = x - 3$

x	y
2	
5	
0	
-2	

4. $y = $ _____

x	y
-5	15
3	7
6	4
-2	12

5. $y = $ _____

x	y
2	9
1	8
-6	1
-2	5

Problem Solving • Reasoning

6. The first two sets of ordered pairs in a function table are (⁻3, ⁻2) and (⁻2, ⁻1). What is the function?

7. If the function is $y = x - 50$ and the first x value is 4, what is the first y value?

_____

_____

Name _____   Date _____

Problem-Solving Skill: Choose an Equation

Choose the equation that describes each situation.

1. As the number of students at Middlecreek Elementary grew, the school hired more teachers.

students	100	200	300	400
teachers	7	12	17	22

a. $s = t + 93$ b. $t = \frac{s}{20} + 2$

c. $s = \frac{t}{20}$

Think: Which equation describes the relationship between the number of students (s) and the number of teachers (t)?

_____

2. Each year, the students at Middlecreek elementary sell candy to raise money for more library books.

students	25	50	75	100
books	105	205	305	405

a. $s = 2b$ b. $b = 4s + 5$

c. $b = s + 90$

Think: Which equation describes the relationship between students (s) and books (b)?

_____

Choose a Strategy

Solve. Use these or other strategies.

Problem-Solving Strategies

• Choose an Equation   • Draw a Diagram   • Use Measurement   • Use Percent

3. Middlecreek Elementary has 400 students. The state average number of students per school is 500. What percent of the state average does Middlecreek have?

_____

4. Middlecreek has 300 students who ride the bus to school each day. West school has $\frac{3}{4}$ as many students who ride the bus as Middlecreek. How many students ride the bus each day at West School?

_____

5. An accountant earns $45,000 per year. How much does she earn in three months?

_____

6. Robert's gross pay was $125. He took home only $95. What percent of his gross pay did he take home?

_____

Name _____   Date _____

Graph an Equation

Find three ordered pairs for each equation. Then use them to
graph the straight line equation.

Example

$$y = x - 2$$

If $x = 5$, $y = 5 - 2 = 3$	(5, 3)
If $x = 3$, $y = 3 - 2 = 1$	(3, 1)
If $x = 0$, $y = 0 - 2 = {}^-2$	(0, 2)

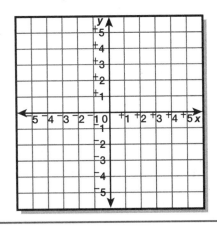

1. $y = x + 5$

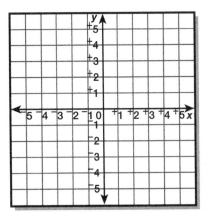

2. $y = 2x - 1$

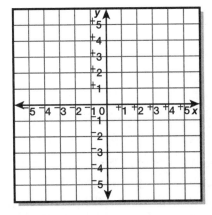

3. $1 - 2x = y$

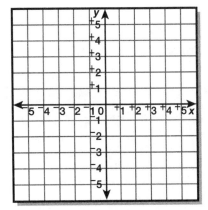

Problem Solving • Reasoning

4. Graph $y = x + 5$ and $y = 3x + 1$. Which
point lies on both lines?

5. Graph the line $y = 2x - 4$. At what point
does the graph cross the y-axis? Why do
you think this happens?

_____   _____

Name _____   Date _____

Problem-Solving Application: Use a Graph

Use a function table and an equation to solve each problem.

1. Students have put bird feeders in the school garden. They see two new types of birds each week. Write an equation to show how many types of birds they will see in week 3, if they saw 2 types of birds the first week.

> **Think:** If you start with the number of weeks (*x*), what operation will you use to get the number of types of birds (*y*)?

_____

2. The students notice that for every 5° over 45°, they see 5 more birds at the feeder. If they see 25 birds when it is 45°, how many birds will they see when it is 55°?

> **Think:** If you start with the temperature (*x*), what operation do you need to get the number of birds (*y*)?

_____

3. The number of pounds of birdseed in the classroom decreases by 3 each week. If the class starts Week 1 with 22 pounds, how much will there be at the beginning of Week 5?

_____

4. The students have predicted that when the temperature goes below 35°F, they will stop seeing many of the birds. If the temperature on October 1st is 55°F and drops 5° every 14 days, when will the temperature be 35°F?

_____

Choose a Strategy

Solve. Choose these or other strategies

Problem-Solving Strategies			
• Use a Graph	• Write an Equation	• Work Backward	• Guess and Check

5. The students bought food to put in the bird feeders. They bought 3 bags of mixed seed at $12.50 per bag, 4 bags of sunflower seed at $15.50 a bag, and 1 bag of premium mix at $20.00 per bag. How much money did the students spend on bird seed?

_____

6. The students hung the bird feeders at various heights in the garden. The highest bird feeder was 10 feet off the ground. The lowest was 75% as high as the highest bird feeder. How high was the lowest bird feeder?

_____